CuteCakes

50 delicious recipes for every occasion

CuteCakes

50 delicious recipes for every occasion

VINCENT SQUARE BOOKS

First published in Great Britain in 2011 by
Vincent Square Books
an imprint of Kyle Books
www.kylebooks.com

ISBN 978 0 85783 046 3

A Cataloguing in Publication record for this title
is available from the British Library.

10 9 8 7 6 5 4 3 2 1

Text copyright © various, see pp.125–126
Photography © various, see pp.127–128
Design © 2011 Kyle Books Limited

Design **Nicky Collings**
Project Editors **Vicky Orchard and Estella Hung**
Production **Nic Jones and David Hearn**

Colour reproduction by Scanhouse in Malaysia
Printed and bound in China by C&C Offset
Printing Co., Ltd

Contents

Introduction

From the classic Madeira Cake (page 30) to the indulgent Chocolate & Brandy Dessert Cake (page 88) and the fruity Mango & Passion Fruit Pavlova (page 106) this is an inspirational collection of cakes for all occasions. There are even gluten-free and vegan options such as Frosted Lemon & Lime Drizzle Cake

(page 45) and Raspberry Buttercream Cake (page 62) to ensure that no-one has to miss out on a delicious slice of something sweet. Throughout the book gluten-free recipes are marked with a GF symbol and vegan ones with a V so they are easy to identify.

Tarts are not only a great option for dessert but also perfect as a snack or even an alternative to a celebratory cake. Choose from zesty Lemon & Raspberry Tart (page 12), Crustless Peach & Almond Pie (page 26) or a slice of classic comfort food in the form of Treacle Star Tart (page 17).

In need of something to accompany your mid-afternoon cup of tea? Then why not try a piece of the tasty but traditional Old-fashioned Victoria Sponge (page 38)? If you're having family and friends round for a more formal afternoon tea then Plum & Almond Butter Cake (page 53) or Warm Marmalade Upside-down Cake (page 51) will never fail to impress your guests. For something more unusual try the Chequerboard Cake (page 32), which tastes as good

as it looks or the Macadamia, Coconut & Pineapple Cake (page 54) for a lovely nutty crunch.

For when you fancy a change from a baked sponge there's a fantastic choice of mouthwatering cheesecakes (Chapter 3) to choose from. From the simple yet sublime Baked Ricotta Cheesecake (page 73) to the luxurious Triple Chocolate Cheesecake (page 77) these are great alternatives to a more traditional pudding to follow your main course. They can can even be served up for festive occasions – the White Christmas Cheesecake (page 70) provides an unusual alternative to the traditional fruit cakes and yule logs.

And who can resist the temptation of a slice of delectable chocolate cake? For all chocoholics there's an inspiring selection of Chocolate Delights (Chapter 4) from the dark and gooey Chocolate Mud Cake (page 87) to the lighter Banana & White Chocolate Cake (page 92). For the more adventurous there's White Chocolate Goat's Cheese Cheesecake (page 95) or Chocolate, Fig & Almond Cake (page 96) for some more unusual flavour combinations.

When you need a cake to celebrate or just to impress then choose something Wildly Decadent (Chapter 5). Chocolate Pistachio Orange Cake (page 100) is full of flavour and looks as appealing as it tastes, while the red and white of the Red Berry Pavlova (page 105) are deliciously dramatic. Angel Cake (page 110) or Tira-Mi-Su Torte (page 115) are great options when you're looking for a birthday cake with a difference while for the festive season there's Panettone (page 116) and, of course, the traditional Christmas cake – Darina Allen's Iced Christmas Cake (page 118).

Hints & tips for perfect cakes every time

It is important to always preheat your oven. This ensures that your cake will be cooked evenly and also that it will be cooked at the correct temperature as soon as it begins baking.

Always grease or line your tart or cake tin with baking parchment. This prevents the cake from sticking and burning.

Make sure your ingredients, particularly dairy (butter, milk, yogurt etc.), and also eggs, are at room temperature before you begin baking.

Pour the prepared cake mix into the centre of the tin and spread the surface evenly with a knife or the back of a spoon. Gently knock the tin to remove any surface air bubbles. It's a good general rule to never fill a cake tin more than half full to prevent spillages.

Place your cake tin in the centre of the oven as this will ensure good circulation of air around the tin during cooking.

Always allow at least half to three quarters of the cooking time to elapse before opening the oven door to check on your cake. Any earlier and you risk the cake sinking.

As the temperature of ovens varies, always check the cake up to 10 minutes before the time given in the recipe. Remove it from the oven if it is done, if not leave in for 2–5 minute intervals at a time, checking after each interval.

To check if a cake is cooked, insert a skewer or cocktail stick into the centre. If it comes out clean, the cake is done, if it has food stuck to it, continue to bake the cake for a few minutes more and repeat the process.

It is a good idea to cool your cake in the tin on a wire rack for 10 minutes before removing from the tin.

Always ensure the cake is completely cool before handling or decorating it to avoid crumbling, breakage or movement of the cake.

If your cake is particularly rounded or uneven, you can level it off with a sharp knife before decorating.

To prevent your cake sticking to the plate or board, dust the surface with icing sugar.

Use a clean pastry brush to clean away any crumbs from the top and sides of your cake before decorating to help ensure a clean surface.

If you are not ready to decorate your cake, wrap in clingfilm and leave in the fridge overnight or place in the freezer until needed. Most cakes can be frozen for up to three months.

Tarts

Lemon & Raspberry Tart

It's hard to beat a wonderfully indulgent lemon and raspberry tart. They look and taste fantastic – a sure-fire way to impress guests.

Makes **1** tart

22–25cm (non-stick) flan case with a removable base and 2cm sides

1 x Sophie Wright's Sweet Pastry (page 121)
butter, for greasing
flour, for rolling

For the filling:
155g caster sugar
6 small or 5 large egg yolks, preferably organic free-range
zest of 4 lemons, juice of 1 lemon
150ml double cream
200g raspberries

icing sugar, for dusting

Put the sweet pastry in the fridge for 30 minutes. To make the tart, grease the flan case with butter on the sides and on the base. Remove the sweet pastry from the fridge. Dust your work surface with plain flour to prevent the pastry from sticking and start to roll it out, turning the pastry every couple of rolls and dusting with extra flour if needed. Roll the pastry to about 2mm thick.

Place the rolling pin at the top end of the rolled-out pastry and roll it around the rolling pin, then move it over to the flan ring and gently lay it into the tin. Don't worry too much if it breaks, you can very easily patch it up with the leftover pastry. Gently press the pastry into the edges of the pastry case (this is important, otherwise it will shrink). Trim off the excess pastry using a knife and leave in the fridge to rest.

Meanwhile, preheat the oven to 180°C/350°F/gas mark 4, and make the filling. Whisk the sugar and egg yolks together until pale white. Use an electric whisk if you prefer. Add the lemon zest and juice.

Heat the cream in a small pan until it starts to boil. Remove it from the heat and slowly pour it over the egg and sugar mix, stirring all the time to prevent it from curdling. Allow to cool slightly.

Remove the pastry case from the fridge and place on a baking tray. Line the pastry with baking parchment, fill it with baking beans and bake blind for 10 minutes. Remove the beans and bake for a further 5 minutes or until the tart case has started to turn slightly golden brown. Scatter the raspberries into the base of the tart case and then pour the lemon cream on the top. Reduce the oven temperature to 160°C/325°F/gas mark 3 and bake the tart for 35 minutes or until the filling is no longer wobbly when gently shaken. Remove from the oven and leave to cool for 1–2 hours. Dust with icing sugar and serve in slices with crème fraîche and fresh raspberries.

Tips: Handle the pastry as little as possible to ensure a better end-product. Also, if you don't rest your pastry it will shrink as you cook it.

Lemongrass, Ginger & Lime Leaf Chocolate Tart

This is such a decadent tart, combining rich dark chocolate spiced up with fragrant lemongrass, lime leaves and ginger. The lychees, filled with white chocolate and chopped lime leaves, add an element of surprise. Raspberries filled with this mix are equally delicious.

Makes tart

For the tart:
275g dark chocolate, broken into small pieces
275ml double cream
4 sticks lemongrass, very finely chopped
3 teaspoons ground ginger
3 Kaffir lime leaves, very finely chopped
juice of 1 lime
6 egg yolks
1 x Maria Elia's Sweet Pastry (page 121)

For the lychees:
250g white chocolate, broken into small pieces
2 Kaffir lime leaves, finely chopped
1 small can lychees
cocoa powder, for dusting

To make the tart, preheat the oven to 180°C/350°F/gas mark 4. Place the chocolate, cream, lemongrass, ginger, lime leaves and lime juice in a heatproof bowl and heat over a pan of barely simmering water until the chocolate has melted. Stir until the mixture is smooth. Remove the bowl from the heat and leave to cool.

Whisk the egg yolks into the chocolate mixture, one at a time. Pour the mixture into the prepared pastry case and cook for 5 minutes, or until just set and shiny. Leave to cool, then refrigerate until about 1 hour before are ready to serve (this is best served at room temperature).

To prepare the lychees, place the white chocolate and lime leaves in a heatproof bowl and heat over a pan of barely simmering water until the chocolate has melted. Remove from the heat and leave to cool until slightly thickened or piping will be difficult.

Spoon the mixture into a small piping bag, and squeeze into the centre of each lychee. Refrigerate until the chocolate has set.

To assemble, dust the tart with cocoa powder and serve with the chocolate lychees.

Treacle Star Tart

This creamy treacle tart is halfway to a pecan pie. Some crème fraîche or a scoop of vanilla ice cream would go down nicely.

Makes 1 tart

23cm x 3–6cm-deep, loose-bottomed tart tin

For the pastry:
230g plain flour
70g golden caster sugar
130g unsalted butter, chilled and diced
1 medium egg, separated
milk

For the filling:
3 medium eggs, plus 2 egg yolks
juice and finely grated zest of 1 lemon
300ml golden syrup
300ml double cream
100g pecan nuts
1 eating apple, peeled and grated
icing sugar for dusting

Put the flour, sugar and butter in a food processor and give it a quick burst at high speed to reduce to a crumb-like consistency. Add the egg yolk and then, with the motor running, trickle in just enough milk for the dough to cling together in lumps. Transfer the pastry to a large bowl and bring it together into a ball with your hands. Wrap the pastry in clingfilm and chill for at least 1 hour, or overnight.

Preheat the oven to 180°C fan/200°C/gas mark 6, and lightly flour the worktop on which to roll out the pastry thinly. Line the cake tin with the pastry. Run a rolling pin across the top and reserve the trimmings. Line the case with foil, fill with baking beans or a dried pulse, and cook for 15 minutes. Remove the foil and beans, paint the case with egg white, patching any cracks with the trimmings, and cook for a further 5–10 minutes until evenly gold. If any cracks have reappeared patch them, then roll out the remaining trimmings slightly thicker than usual, and cut out 6 star shapes 6cm in diameter.

Turn the oven down to 150°C fan/170°C/gas mark 3. Whisk together the eggs, yolks, lemon juice and zest, add the golden syrup and cream and whisk until the mixture emulsifies. Finely chop the pecan nuts in the food processor, add to the mixture with the grated apple and mix well. Pour the mixture into the tart case, and decorate with the pastry stars. Place it on a baking tray and bake for 60 minutes. The filling should be lightly golden, puffy at the edges. Remove and leave the tart to cool for a couple of hours. Just before serving, dust with icing sugar.

Plum, Blueberry & Almond Tart

Serve this recipe with chilled crème fraîche to balance the sweetness of the tart.

Makes **1** tart

500g block of frozen,
    all-butter puff pastry,
    defrosted
flour, for rolling pastry
    milk, for brushing pastry
250g block of white marzipan
400g plums, halved and
    stoned
25g butter
125g blueberries
4 tablespoons Plum &
    Blueberry Jam (see below)
25g flaked almonds

Preheat the oven to 200°C/400°F/gas mark 6. Roll out the pastry on a floured surface until it forms a rectangle measuring about 29cm x 37cm. Trim a 2cm wide strip from all the edges and reserve. Place the pastry rectangle on to a baking sheet. Brush the edges with milk, then stick the strips all around the outside of the rectangle, trimming as necessary. Prick the base of the pastry with a fork.

Roll out the marzipan very thinly, then place it on to the pastry rectangle and, using both hands, pull it so that it sits inside the pastry case, scrunching it up a little so that it looks like an unmade bed. Scatter the plum halves over the top, cut-side up, and dot them with the butter. Scatter over the blueberries. (If you wish, you can make the tart up to this stage and keep it in the fridge overnight.)

Warm the jam with 3 tablespoons water to make it a little runnier, then drizzle half over the fruit. Scatter over the almonds and brush the exposed pastry edges with a little milk. Bake for 20 minutes. Remove the tart from the oven, drizzle over the remaining jam and return it to the oven for a further 10–15 minutes, or until the pastry is golden and the plums are tender. Serve warm or cold with crème fraîche.

Plum & Blueberry Jam

Makes about 3 litres
Keeps for at least a year

2.5kg ripe red plums, stone
    and chopped into
    bite-sized pieces
250g blueberries
juice of 4 lemons
2kg jam sugar

Stir all the ingredients together in a bowl. Leave the mixture to macerate in the bowl for 2 hours, which will give the fruit time to release its juices. Transfer the fruit to a pan and cook gently, until the plums have wrinkled and softened a little and the mixture has begun to rise in the pan. Increase the heat and boil for a further 15-20 minutes, or until the jam has reached setting point. Remove the pan from the heat and leave to cool for 10 minutes, then pour the jam into sterilised jars and seal.

Toffeed Apple & Pecan Tart

This tart tastes best if made on the day of serving, but well in advance giving you time to chill it in the refrigerator for at least 3 hours. This firms up the filling giving a toffee-like quality.

Makes **1** tart

23cm fluted tart tin

200g Pâte Sucrée
  (see below)
2 small eggs beaten
150g butter
150g light brown sugar
75ml double cream
150g pecan nuts
2 small dessert apples

200ml double cream

Preheat the oven to 180°C/350°F/gas mark 4.

Roll out the pastry and use to line the tart tin. Bake blind. Use a little of the beaten egg to brush the tart case. Cook for 1 minute, then brush again and cook for a further minute.

Place the butter, sugar and cream in a pan large enough to take all the filling ingredients. Cook slowly to dissolve the sugar, bring to the boil and cook, stirring, for 1 minute. Remove from the heat and stir in the pecan nuts. Allow to cool slightly.

Peel and core the apples and cut into 1cm dice. Stir into the toffee mixture along with the beaten egg. Spoon into the prepared pastry case and bake for 20–25 minutes. Leave to cool and serve with double cream.

Pâte Sucrée (sweet shortcrust pastry)

200g plain flour
pinch of salt
50g caster sugar
100g butter
2 egg yolks
1 teaspoon vanilla extract
1 tablespoon water

Sift the flour and salt on to a large clean area of your work surface. A piece of marble is perfect, but not essential, for making pastry as it keeps everything cool. With a ramekin or small bowl work the flour from the centre in a circular motion, to create a large well. Keep going until you have a ring of flour approximately 46cm in diameter. Sprinkle the sugar just inside the flour to give an inner, slightly smaller ring.

Soften the butter and break it into small pieces, place in the centre of the ring along with the egg yolks, vanilla extract and water.

Using your fingers or, of you have one, a plastic baker's card, work the eggs and butter until they resemble fine scrambled eggs.

Bring in the sugar and work briefly. Using the baker's card or a palette knife bring in all the flour, chopping and churning the butter as you go. Continue chopping and turning until everything is well mixed and close to coming together. Now is the time to add a little more water if you think the dough is going to be too dry. You'll usually find it is not required.

This is the fun part: using the heel of your hand lightly push the dough down and away from you. Do this thoroughly but once only; overworking will only make the pastry tough. Now bring the dough together and work lightly into a ball. Wrap in greaseproof paper or clingfilm and refrigerate for 30 minutes before using, or wrap well and freeze until required.

Strawberry Tart

This summer tart is lovely for an al fresco summer lunch. Both the tart and the custard can be made in advance, only leaving the assembly to the last minute.

Makes **1** tart

23 cm round, loose-bottomed tart tin

200g pastry
200ml milk
1 vanilla pod, split
3 egg yolks
60g caster sugar
30g plain flour
900g strawberries
redcurrant jelly

For the pastry:
200g plain flour
pinch of salt
100g butter
1 teaspoon vanilla essence
45g icing sugar
2 egg yolks
1 dessertspoon water
1 egg, beaten

To make the pastry, sift the flour and salt into a food-processor. Add the diced butter and vanilla essence and process until the mixture resembles fine breadcrumbs. Sift in the icing sugar and add the egg yolks along with the cold water. Process to a smooth dough. Wrap in clingfilm and chill for at least 1 hour.

Preheat the oven to 180°C/350°F/gas mark 4.

On a lightly floured surface roll the dough to a circle and use to line the tart tin. Prick the base and bake blind for 10 minutes. Remove the baking beans and cook for a further 10 minutes. Brush the base and sides of the pastry case with beaten egg and return to the oven for 1 minute. Repeat once more. Cool.

Place the milk and split vanilla pod in a small pan and bring to the boil. Meanwhile, whisk together the yolks and sugar until thick and pale. Stir in the flour. Pour a little of the hot milk on to the yolks, stir to blend and then return to the pan to cook. When boiling point is reached, reduce the heat and cook for 1 more minute. This type of thickened custard will not separate as the flour binds it, although it has a tendency to stick to the pan so stir and whisk it continually. Transfer to a bowl to cool. Dab the top with a little melted butter to prevent a skin from forming.

When the tart case and custard are both cold, and no more than 1–2 hours before you are ready to serve, remove the vanilla pod, scraping the seeds into the custard as you do so. Beat the custard to ensure it is smooth, then spoon into the pastry case and spread to level.

Wipe and hull the strawberries and arrange on top of the custard. Warm the redcurrant jelly and brush evenly over the fruit to give a wonderful glaze.

Dutch Apple Pie

Dutch apple pie has been around for centuries – probably because it's hard not to love the flavourings of cinnamon and lemon juice with the tart apples.

Makes **1** tart   **V** Vegan

For the crust:
75g non-hydrogenated vegetable margarine
165g unbleached plain flour
¼ teaspoon salt
4 tablespoons cold water

For the apple filling:
6 large Granny Smith apples, peeled, cored and slice into 5mm thick pieces
35g unbleached plain flour
130g evaporated cane juice (use organic whole cane sugar if this is not available)
2 teaspoons cinnamon

For the crumb topping:
130g unbleached plain flour
100g soft light brown sugar
70g butter substitute

Preheat the oven to 220°C/425°F/gas mark 7. To make the crust, use a standing mixer on medium speed, beat the shortening until smooth. Scrape down the sides of the bowl and add the flour and salt. While the mixer is still running, add the cold water one tablespoon at a time until a dough starts to form. Blend the mixture until just combined, 30 seconds. (Blending too much will make the dough tough.) On a lightly floured work surface, roll out the dough to 5mm thick. Roll the dough on to a rolling pin and unroll it into a pie dish. Crimp the edges of the dough and set aside.

Now make the apple filling. In a large bowl, mix the flour, cane juice and cinnamon with the apple slices and set aside.

For the crumb topping, use a stand mixer to combine the flour and brown sugar. While the mixer is still running, add the butter substitute 1 tablespoon at a time. Mix until the crumb topping resembles very coarse sand.

Spoon the apples from the large bowl into the pie crust, making sure not to get the liquid from the bowl into the pie crust (this will help the pie to stay together once cut). Top with all the crumb topping. Place the pie dish on a foil-lined baking sheet for easy cleaning. Cover the pie with foil and bake for 35 minutes. Reduce the heat to 180°C/350°F/gas mark 4, remove the foil, and bake for 10 more minutes to brown the topping and crust. Cool on a wire rack for 1 hour. Lightly cover and store at room temperature.

ss Peach
nd Pie

...many other fruits can be used for this dessert, such as pears, apples, figs, apricots or plums. It is very good served hot but even better just slightly warm. Serve with crème fraîche or cream.

Makes **1** tart

22.5cm deep flan dish, greased

8 large peaches or nectarines
2–3 tablespoons ground almonds or breadcrumbs, for coating
3 tablespoons apricot jam, sieved
crème fraîche or cream, to serve (optional)

For the filling:
150g softened butter
75g caster sugar
1 teaspoon grated orange rind
1 teaspoon grated lemon rind
3 eggs
150g ground almonds
3 tablespoons plain flour
a few drops of almond essence
2 teaspoons orange-blossom water
2 tablespoons orange liqueur

Preheat the oven to 200°C/400°F/gas mark 6.

First make the filling. Put the butter and sugar into the bowl of your mixer and whisk at high speed for 1 minute or until the butter is light and fluffy. Gradually add the remaining filling ingredients, and mix to a smooth cream.

If peaches are used, plunge them into boiling water, lift out, refresh with iced water and peel. Nectarines do not need peeling. Halve the fruit, remove the stones and cut into thin slices.

Sprinkle the ground almonds or breadcrumbs on the baking dish, and knock out the excess. Pour the creamed mixture into the dish and spread out evenly with a small spatula or the back of a spoon. Arrange the sliced fruit on top in a decorative pattern.

Bake for 15–20 minutes or until set. Meanwhile, in a small saucepan, melt the apricot jam together with 2 tablespoons water. Bring to the boil. Use to brush over the flan as soon as it comes out of the oven. Either serve hot or just warm with a dollop of crème fraîche, double cream or, best of all, fresh clotted cream.

Afternoon Tea Cakes

Madeira Cake

This traditional firm yet light sponge cake requires only a handful of ingredients and is easy to whip up to accompany an afternoon cup of tea.

Makes **1** cake

18cm x 7.5cm-deep round cake tin

175g soft butter
175g caster sugar
3 organic eggs
½ teaspoon pure vanilla extract
225g plain white flour
½ teaspoon baking powder
1 tablespoon milk or water

Preheat the oven to 180°C/350°F/gas mark 4. Line the base and side of the cake tin with greaseproof paper.

Cream the butter in a mixing bowl with a wooden spoon, add the caster sugar and whisk until light and fluffy. This will give you a lighter, smoother cake than just dumping the sugar in with the butter at the beginning. Better still, cream the butter and sugar with your hand in the time-honoured, old-fashioned way; it will cream faster from the heat of your hand and produce a light cake.

Whisk together the eggs and vanilla extract and gradually add to the creamed butter and sugar. Whisk well. If preferred, the eggs may be whisked into the mixture one at a time, and a little sieved flour may be added between each addition of egg. Fold in the remainder of the flour, adding the baking powder mixed in with the last addition of the flour. Add a little water or milk if necessary, to make a dropping consistency. Fill into the prepared cake tin.

Bake for about 50–60 minutes, remove from the oven and leave to cool in the tin.

Chequerboard Cake

Don't be afraid: like so many of the pastry chef's techniques, this cake is incredibly easy once you know what to do.

Makes **1** cake

3 x 20cm square cake tins
2 x pastry bags with 2.25cm plain or fluted nozzles

For the vanilla batter:
225g unsalted butter
225g caster sugar
4 large eggs
1 teaspoon vanilla extract
250g plain flour
10g baking powder

For the chocolate batter:
225g unsalted butter
225g caster sugar
4 large eggs
220g plain flour
50g cocoa powder
10g baking powder

For the sugar syrup:
250g granulated sugar
300ml water
1 tablespoon rum
2 tablespoons apricot jam

For the ganache:
150g good-quality dark chocolate, minimum 60 per cent cocoa solids, broken into pieces
150ml whipping cream

Preheat the oven to 190°C/375°F/gas mark 5. Butter the cake tins, line the bases with rounds of waxed paper, then butter the paper. Begin by making the sugar syrup. Put the sugar and water in a saucepan and bring to the boil, without stirring, and boil until it begins to thicken. Remove from the heat and add the rum. Set aside.

To make the vanilla batter, cream together the butter and caster sugar thoroughly. Add the eggs, one by one, mixing well between each addition, then add the vanilla extract. Sift together the flour and baking powder and add to the mixture, stirring well. The mixture will be quite stiff. Set aside while you make the second batch.

To make the chocolate batter, cream together the butter and the caster sugar thoroughly. Add the eggs one by one, mixing well between each addition. Sift together the flour, cocoa and the baking powder and add to the mixture, stirring well. The mixture will be quite stiff.

Place the piping nozzles securely in the pastry bags. Put all the vanilla mixture into one of the bags and the chocolate mixture into the other. Place the three prepared baking tins in a row.

Starting with the vanilla batter, pipe a ring of vanilla batter inside the outer rim of one of the cake tins. Then pipe a ring of chocolate batter inside the vanilla ring. Continue to pipe alternating rings of vanilla and chocolate batter. There should be 6 rings of alternating batter, the centre one being chocolate. Fill the second cake pan in the same way.

Fill the third cake tin, starting with a chocolate ring and ending with a vanilla ring. Tap the base of each of the cake tins gently on a flat surface to release any air pockets before placing in the oven. Bake for about 20 minutes.

Remove the cakes from the oven, leave in their tins for 5 minutes to cool slightly. Turn them out on to a wire cooling rack and brush the sugar syrup over the bottom of each cake. Allow to cool.

To make the ganache, melt the chocolate in a heatproof bowl suspended over a saucepan of barely simmering water. Set aside.

Whip the cream until soft peaks form, then pour the hot chocolate over it in a steady stream, continuing to whip the cream, until the chocolate is just blended.

Once cool, place one of the cakes with a vanilla outer ring on a serving plate, spread apricot jam over the cake and then place the cake that has the chocolate outer ring on top of it. Spread apricot jam over it, then place the third cake on the top. Using a palette knife, spread the ganache over the top and sides of the cake to cover it completely.

Coffee Cake

This coffee cake is great for all occasions and the buttercream filling and glacéicing add a complementary contrast in textures.

Makes **1** cake

2 x 20cm sandwich tins

225g butter
225g caster sugar
4 organic eggs
225g white flour
1 teaspoon baking powder
4–5 tablespoons coffee
essence

For the coffee buttercream filling:
50g butter
110g icing sugar, sieved
1–2 teaspoons coffee
essence

For the coffee glacé icing:
225g icing sugar
scant 1 tablespoon coffee
essence
about 2 tablespoons boiling
water

For decoration:
hazelnuts or chocolate
coffee beans

Preheat the oven to 180°C/350°F/gas mark 4. Brush the tins with melted butter, dust with flour and line the base of each with a disc of greaseproof paper. Brush with melted butter.

Cream the butter until soft, add the caster sugar and beat until pale and light in texture. Whisk the eggs, and add to the mixture bit by bit, beating well between each addition. Sift together the flour and the baking powder and stir gently into the cake mixture, finally adding in the coffee essence. Mix thoroughly.

Spoon the mixture into the prepared sandwich tins and bake for about 30 minutes in the oven. When the cakes are cooked, the centre will be firm and springy and the edges will have slightly shrunk from the sides of the tin.

Allow to rest in the tin for a few minutes before turning out on to the wire rack. Remove the greaseproof paper from the base, then reinvert so the top of the cakes don't get marked by the wire rack. Cool the cakes on the wire rack.

To make the coffee buttercream filling, beat the butter with the icing sugar and the coffee essence.

To make the coffee glacé icing, sift the icing sugar into a bowl, and add the coffee essence and enough boiling water to make it the consistency of thick cream.

When cold, sandwich the cakes together with the filling and spread the icing over the top. Decorate with hazelnuts or chocolate coffee beans.

Porter Cake

Porter cake made with the black stout of Ireland is now an established Irish cake, rich and moist with 'plenty of cutting'. Either Guinness, Murphy's or Beamish stouts can be used, depending on where your loyalties are.

Makes **1** cake

20 x 7cm-deep round cake tin, lined with greaseproof paper

450g plain white flour
pinch of salt
1 level teaspoon baking powder
225g caster sugar
1 level teaspoon freshly grated nutmeg
1 level teaspoon mixed spice
225g butter
450g sultanas
50g candied peel (see page 119)
50g glacé cherries
300ml porter or stout
2 organic eggs, beaten

Preheat the oven to 180°C/350°F/gas mark 4.

Sieve the flour, salt and baking powder into a bowl, and add the sugar, nutmeg and spice. Rub in the butter. Add the fruit, then mix the porter with the beaten eggs. Pour into the other ingredients and mix well.

Turn into the lined tin and bake for about 2 hours. Allow to cool in the tin, wrap in silicone paper and keep for several days before cutting to allow the cake to mature.

Old-fashioned Victoria Sponge

When fresh strawberries aren't in season, just use strawberry jam instead.

Makes **1** cake

3 x 18cm sandwich tins, greased and lined with greaseproof paper

220g butter, plus extra for greasing
220g caster sugar
4 eggs
220g self-raising flour
pinch of salt
2 tablespoons warm water
200ml whipped cream
300g strawberries, hulled and sliced
icing sugar, for dusting

Preheat the oven to 190°C/375°F/gas mark 5.

In a large bowl, cream together the butter and sugar using a wooden spoon or an electric mixer. Beat in the eggs one at a time.

Sift the flour and salt into a bowl, add the warm water, and mix well.

Transfer to the prepared tins and bake for 15–20 minutes. Let cool.

Place one of the sponges on a cake stand and spread over half of the whipped cream followed by half of the sliced strawberries. Place another sponge on top and repeat, finishing with the third sponge on the top.

Dust with icing sugar.

Citrus Frosted Carrot Cake

This delicious moist cake keeps really well and can be frozen without the frosting. If you don't like walnuts, omit them or replace with hazelnuts.

Makes **1** cake

23cm loose-bottomed cake tin, lined with greaseproof paper, lightly dusted with flour

275g self-raising flour
1 teaspoon baking powder
1 teaspoon bicarbonate soda
1 rounded teaspoon cinnamon
½ teaspoon salt
zest of 1 lemon
50g chopped walnuts
175g caster sugar
3 eggs
175g butter, melted and cooled
300g grated carrots
1 large or 2 small bananas, mashed

For the frosting:
150g cream cheese
40–50g icing sugar
juice and zest of ½ lemon

a few walnut halves
   (optional)

Preheat the oven to 180°C/350°F/gas mark 4.

Sift the flour into a large bowl with the baking powder, bicarbonate of soda and cinnamon. Add the salt, lemon zest, nuts and sugar. Beat the eggs and add to the bowl along with the butter, carrots and banana. Stir thoroughly until everything is well mixed. Pour into the prepared tin and bake for approximately 45 minutes. The cake will be risen and golden and a skewer inserted will come out clean.

Leave the cake to cool in the tin for 10 minutes, then remove from the tin and leave to cool completely on a wire rack.

To make the frosting, soften the cream cheese in a bowl. Add the icing sugar, lemon juice and zest to taste. Spread the frosting evenly over the top of the cake and decorate with walnut halves if desired.

Seville Orange Marmalade Cake

When fresh out of the oven, this cake makes a gorgeous pudding with a blob of crème fraîche, but it also keeps well.

Makes **1** cake

17 x 7.5cm-deep cake tin, lined with silicone paper

350g self-raising flour
pinch of salt
150g butter
150g caster sugar
4 tablespoons Seville Orange
    Marmalade (see below)
    the peel chopped; plus 2–3
    extra tablespoons for the
    topping
2 organic eggs, lightly beaten
5 tablespoons full cream milk
icing sugar, for dusting

Preheat the oven to 180°C/350°F/gas mark 4.

Sift the flour and salt into a bowl, rub in the butter and add the sugar. Make a well in the centre, add the 4 tablespoons of marmalade and the eggs and mix to a softish consistency with the milk.

Put into the cake tin and bake for about 1¼ hours. Then remove from the oven and leave to cool on a wire tray. Generously paint the top with marmalade and dust with icing sugar.

Seville Whole Orange Marmalade

Makes about 5.8-6.75kg

2.25kg Seville or Malaga
    oranges
4kg sugar, warmed

Put the oranges in a stainless steel saucepan with 5.2 litres of water. Put a plate on top of the oranges to keep them under the surface of the water. Cover the saucpan, then simmer gently until the oranges are soft, about 2 hours. Cool and drain, reserving the water. (If more convenient, leave overnight and continue the next day.)

Put a chopping board onto a large baking tray with sides so you won't lose any juice. Then cut the oranges in half and scoop out the soft centre. Slice the peel finely and put the pips into a muslin bag. Put the escaped juice, sliced oranges and the muslin bag of pips into a large, wide stainless steel saucepan with the reserved cooking liquid. Bring to the boil, reduce by half or, better still, two-thirds. Add the warmed sugar and stir over a brisk heat until dissolved. Boil fast until setting point is reached. Pot in sterilised jars and cover immediately. Store in a dark, airy cupboard.

Frosted Lemon & Lime Drizzle Cake

Use lemon and lime syrup to moisten the sponge and a thin lime fondant glaze to finish the cake off, which gives a really zingy flavour.

Makes **1** cake **GF** Gluten-free

20cm round, loose-bottomed cake tin, greased and lined with baking parchment

vegetable oil, for oiling
225g caster sugar
4 medium eggs, at room temperature
350g Phil Vickery's Gluten-free Flour (page 121)
1½ teaspoons xanthan gum
2 teaspoons baking powder
400ml semi-skimmed milk
200ml sunflower oil
zest and juice of 2 large lemons

For the syrup:
2 large limes
75g granulated sugar

For the crunchy icing:
juice of 1 large lime
100g fondant icing sugar
granulated sugar, for sprinkling
zest of lemon and lime, to decorate

Preheat the oven to 180°C/350°F/gas mark 4.

Whisk together the sugar and the eggs in a food-processor until thick and creamy. Sift together the flour, xanthan gum and baking powder to combine evenly and add this to the sugar and eggs. Whisk in the milk, oil and lemon zest (reserve the juice for the syrup).

Spoon the mixture into the prepared tin and bake for about 30 minutes, until firm and springy in the centre. Test with a skewer; if it comes out clean, it's done. The cake will be nicely browned and domed. Once cooked, remove from the oven and allow it to cool slightly in the tin.

To make the syrup, squeeze the limes and pour the juice into a measuring jug with the reserved lemon juice – you'll need approximately 120ml in total. Next, place the measured lemon and lime juice into a small pan with the granulated sugar and boil them together for 1 minute.

Prick the warm cake all over with a skewer, while it is still in the tin, then pour over the hot syrup. Once the cake is cool, carefully remove it from the tin and place it on a wire rack to cool completely.

To make the icing, place the lime juice in a small bowl and add the fondant icing sugar to form a runny icing. Sprinkle the top of the cake with a little granulated sugar. Pour the icing all over the cake and leave to run over the edge. Decorate with lemon and lime zest.

To store: The iced cake keeps well for 2 days in an airtight container in the fridge.

To freeze: The un-iced cake freezes well. Wrap the cake in baking parchment and place in an airtight container. Store for up to 3 months.

Somerset Apple Cake

Somerset, Dorset and Kent all have traditional apple cake recipes. This one is more or less a combination of all three, but is most like the one found in Somerset. Only the addition of black treacle makes it different – it imparts not only a rich caramel taste, but also a good dark colour. Serve the cake with Greek yogurt or thick cream.

Makes **1** cake

24cm loose-bottomed cake tin, base-lined and greased

170g unsalted butter, softened
170g soft light brown sugar
3 eggs, beaten
1 tablespoon black treacle
227g wholemeal flour
113g self-raising flour
1 teaspoon mixed spice
1 teaspoon ground cinnamon
680g cooking apples, peeled
   about 3 tablespoons milk
caster sugar, to dust

Preheat the oven to 160°C/325°F/gas mark 3.

Cream the butter and sugar together until light and fluffy. Beat in the eggs, a little at a time, with the black treacle. Sift the flours and spices into a bowl and stir well.

Cut the apples into chunks and add to the mixture, with just enough milk to combine to a soft, dropping consistency. Turn into the prepared tin and bake for about 1¼ hours or until a skewer inserted into the middle comes out clean.

Sprinkle with caster sugar, then set on a wire rack. Allow to cool in the tin. Serve warm.

Vanilla & Raspberry Cake

Sed id mi odio. Morbi viverra, velit sed suscipit lacinia, arcu quam mattis mauris, consequat commodo nisi turpis ut mi. Phasellus placerat metus sed justo faucibus.

Makes **1** cake **GF** Gluten-free

20cm round Victorian sandwich tins, greased and lined with baking parchment

For the sponge:
vegetable oil, for greasing
350g golden caster sugar
4 medium eggs, at room temperature
2 teaspoons vanilla extract
2 teaspoons glycerine
350g Phil Vickery's Gluten-free Flour Mix (page 121)
1 teaspoon xanthan gum
3 teaspoons baking powder
250ml semi-skimmed milk
250 sunflower oil

For the buttercream and decoration:
225g unsalted butter, softened
225g icing sugar, sieved
1 teaspoon vanilla extract
4 tablespoons raspberry jam
fresh raspberries
edible glitter

Preheat the oven to 180°C/350°F/gas mark 4.

Put the caster sugar, eggs, vanilla extract and glycerine into a food mixer and whisk on high speed for 3 minutes. Sift together the flour, xanthan gum and baking powder to combine evenly. In a jug, mix the milk with the oil.

When the eggs are nice and thick, add the flour mix. Return the bowl to the mixer and slowly add the milk and the oil. Whisk thoroughly, but don't go mad.

Divide the mixture evenly between the tins and level the surface. Bake on the same shelf in the centre of the oven for 30–35 minutes until golden and firm. The cakes are ready when a skewer inserted into the sponge comes out clean.

Leave the cakes to cool in the tins for 15 minutes and then turn out on to a wire rack to cool completely. Peel off the lining paper and decorate the cakes or freeze them (see opposite) until you are ready to use them.

To make the buttercream, beat the butter with the icing sugar and vanilla extract until light and fluffy.

Select the cake with the best top and set it aside. Turn the other cake over (trim the base to make it sit flat if necessary) and place it on a serving plate or cake board. Spread a layer of buttercream over the base sponge, saving a generous amount for the top. Spread the same sponge with raspberry jam and sandwich the two cakes together.

Spread the rest of the buttercream over the top of the cake. Top with fresh raspberries and sprinkle with some edible glitter. The cake is best eaten on the same day that you ice and decorate it.

Filling variations: Buttercream and jam are a classic combination for filling a sponge cake but you could also use lightly whipped cream with crushed fresh berries, or if the mood takes you, try lemon curd or marmalade and liqueur instead.

To store: The un-iced cakes will keep for 2 days in an airtight container.

To freeze: Wrap the cooled sponges in clingfilm and store in the freezer for up to 3 months. Fill and ice the cake once it has defrosted.

Roasted Banana
Walnut Cake with Maple Icing

This recipe combines irresistable flavours in one moist sponge cake. It is made with roasted bananas for a great texture, and drizzled with a deliciously sticky maple icing – fantastic!

Makes **1** cake **GF** Gluten-free

23cm x 13cm x 7cm loaf tin

vegetable oil, for oiling
450g bananas with skin on
   (about 250g after roasting)
150g light muscovado sugar
125ml sunflower oil
1 teaspoon glycerine
3 medium eggs, at room
   temperature
225g Phil Vickery's Gluten-
   Free Flour Mix B (page 121)
½ teaspoon xanthan gum
½ teaspoon bicarbonate of
   soda
½ teaspoon baking powder
2 tablespoons crème fraîche
   or cream cheese
50g walnut pieces

For the maple icing:
3 tablespoons maple syrup
75g fondant icing sugar
crushed walnuts, to decorate

Preheat the oven to 200°C/400°F/gas mark 6. Make a slit in each banana and place on a baking tray. Roast the bananas in their skins for about 10 minutes until soft. Cool, mash roughly, and set aside.

Reduce the oven temperature to 180°C/350°F/gas mark 4. Oil the loaf tin and line the base with baking parchment. Tip the sugar into a large mixing bowl and, using a hand-held electric mixer, whisk in the oil, glycerine and eggs, one at a time.

Sift together the flour, xanthan gum, bicarbonate of soda and baking powder and mix this into the bowl, with the crème fraîche or cream cheese. Stir in 250g mashed banana and the walnuts and mix all the ingredients thoroughly.

Smooth the mixture into the prepared tin and bake for about 45 minutes until firm and springy when touched. Test with a skewer, which should come out clean when inserted into the centre. Cool in the tin for 10 minutes. Turn the cake out of the tin, peel off the paper and cool on a wire rack.

For the icing, mix the maple syrup into the fondant icing, with just enough drops of water to make a runny icing. Set the cake on a serving plate, drizzle the maple glaze over and scatter some crushed walnuts on the top. Cut into slices to serve.

To store: The un-iced cake will keep for 1 week in an airtight container.

To freeze: Wrap the un-iced cake in baking parchment and foil and freeze in an airtight container. Defrost for 1–2 hours and ice after defrosting.

Plum & Almond Butter Cake

This is a buttery sponge cake with moist, sweet fruit, to cut into wedges. Try it in autumn when plums are in season. Alternatively choose cherries, peaches, nectarines or apricots in the summer months. This cake can be warmed before serving and enjoyed as a dessert with ice cream or served cold – and it's great for picnics.

Makes **1** cake **GF** Gluten-free

20cm round cake tin

vegetable oil, for oiling
3 medium eggs, at room
   temperature
2 teaspoons vanilla extract
125g caster sugar
200g Phil Vickery's Gluten-
   Free Flour Mix B (page 121)
1 tablespoon baking powder
1 teaspoon xanthan gum
125g unsalted butter, melted
1 teaspoon glycerine
3 tablespoons semi-skimmed
   milk
350–400g red plums,
   quartered and stoned
2 tablespoons demerara
   sugar
125g flaked almonds

Preheat the oven to 180°C/350°F/gas mark 4. Oil the cake tin and line the base with baking parchment.

Put the eggs into a bowl with the vanilla extract and caster sugar. Using a hand-held electric mixer, whisk until light and the mixture forms a trail. Sift the flour with the baking powder and xanthan gum, mix thoroughly and fold into the mixture, stirring lightly, so you don't lose all the air in the batter. Stir in the melted butter, glycerine and milk. Do not overbeat.

Put a layer of cake mixture in the base of the tin. Scatter some of the plums over, then spoon in the rest of the cake batter. Tip the remaining plums on top. Sprinkle the demerara sugar and almonds over the fruit.

Place the cake on a baking tray and bake for about 45 minutes, until the plums have begun to caramelise and a skewer inserted into the cake comes out clean. Remove the cake from the oven, leave to cool slightly and then gently loosen the sides. Transfer to a wire rack to cool completely.

To store: The cake will keep for 1 week in an airtight container.

To freeze: Wrap the cake in baking parchment and foil, and freeze in an airtight container.

Macadamia, Coconut & Pineapple Cake

The macadamia nuts give this cake a nice crunch and a good buttery flavour since the cake is made without any butter or oil.

Makes **1** cake

2 x 20cm sandwich tins

142g golden caster sugar
3 eggs
85g macadamia nuts,
    roughly chopped
1 x 400g can of crushed
    pineapple (in natural juice)
142g self-raising flour, sifted
85g desiccated coconut

For the filling and topping:
227g mascarpone cream
    cheese
about 2 tablespoons of
    pineapple juice, from the
    can
28g shredded coconut or
    coconut chips

Preheat the oven to 180°C/350°F/gas mark 4. Using a balloon whisk, beat together the sugar and eggs until thick and creamy, then stir in the chopped nuts. Strain the pineapple, reserving the juice. Add to the bowl, stirring well to combine. Fold in the flour and coconut and gently mix together. Spoon into the prepared sandwich tins and smooth the tops.

Bake for about 20 minutes or until golden brown on top and springy to the touch in the centre. Leave to cool in the tins for 5 minutes before transferring to a wire rack to cool completely.

Meanwhile, toast the shredded coconut or coconut chips. Spread on a baking tray and set under a preheated grill for 2–3 minutes, or until golden brown. Watch them carefully and remove immediately when they start to colour.

To make the filling, beat the mascarpone cheese until smooth, then mix with a little of the reserved pineapple juice – the consistency should be neither too thick nor too runny. Make sure the 2 cakes are completely cold before using half the mixture to sandwich them together. Spread the rest over the top. Decorate with the toasted coconut. To serve, cut into thin slices.

Cranberry Strussel Cake

Most cranberries come from North America, the vast bogs of New England to be precise. Water is flooded into the bogs, the cranberries mechanically detached and float to form a sea of scarlet berries. Dried cranberries are widely available in supermarkets; they are extremely tasty and make original additions to mixed dried fruit compotes.

Makes **1** cake

22cm springform tin, greased and floured

100g plain flour
100g light muscovado sugar
1 teaspoon mixed spice
75g butter, melted
50g flaked almonds
100g butter, softened
200g self-raising flour
200g light muscovado sugar
2 eggs, beaten
100ml sour cream
200g cranberries
zest of 1 orange
1 tablespoon light
   muscovado sugar
300g cranberries
2 oranges, zest of 1, juice of
   both
75g light muscovado
   sugar
whipped cream
icing sugar

Preheat the oven to 200°C/400°F/gas mark 6.

Sieve the flour, muscovado sugar and mixed spices into a mixing bowl, pour over the melted butter and mix in with a fork. You should end up with a crumbly mixture. Stir in the flaked almonds and set aside. This is the strussel topping.

Put the softened butter in a bowl, sift in the flour and second batch of muscovado sugar, then add the eggs and sour cream. Beat with an electric whisk for 1 minute or so, until a smooth batter is formed. Spoon into the prepared tin and level the top.

Wash the cranberries and dry them well. Place them in an even layer over the cake mixture. Sprinkle the orange zest and a little muscovado sugar over the fruit. Spoon over the prepared strussel topping and bake for 30 minutes or until a skewer inserted in the centre of the cake comes out clean. The cake should be risen and golden.

Whilst the cake is cooking, prepare the compote. Place the remaining cranberries in a pan, add the orange zest and juice and the remaining muscovado sugar. Cook slowly for 6–7 minutes until the fruits begin to pop and burst; let some remain whole. Transfer to a bowl.

Serve the cake dusted with a little icing sugar accompanied by the cranberry compote and a bowl of whipped cream.

Cinnamon Spice Plum Cake

A delicious way to use plums.

Makes **1** cake

20cm springform tin, greased
  and lined with greaseproof
  paper

110g unsalted butter,
  softened
200g caster sugar
2 eggs
190g plain flour
1 teaspoon baking powder
pinch of salt
1 teaspoon grated lemon
  zest
1 tablespoon lemon juice
3 tablespoons milk
6 plums, halved and pitted
2 teaspoons ground
  cinnamon

Preheat the oven to 180°C/350°F/gas mark 4.

Whisk together the butter and all but 2 tablespoons of the sugar and butter mixture. Once mixed, sift the flour, baking powder and salt into a bowl along with the lemon zest, juice and milk and fold through. Pour into the prepared tin.

Toss the plum halves in the remaining sugar, together with the cinnamon, then place gently, cut side down, on top of the cake mixture. Cook for about 50 minutes, until a skewer when inserted in the centre of the cake comes out clean. Leave to cool slightly before removing from the tin.

Cut into wedges.

Warm Marmalade Upside-down Cake

This is particularly tasty when served with a dollop of crème fraîche. Use any kind of marmalade you like, except perhaps a dark one, as it would conceal the pretty oranges arranged on the top. Try it also with halved apricots or plums (and the jam equivalent) in the summer or autumn.

Makes **1** cake

22.5cm x 6cm deep round springform cake tin, greased

For the base:
40g butter
40g caster sugar
2 heaped tablespoons marmalade of choice
2–3 large sweet oranges, peeled, pith and pips removed, and sliced very thinly

For the cake:
200g very soft butter
4 large eggs, at room temperature
3 heaped tablespoons of marmalade of choice
2 tablespoons milk
17g caster sugar
200g self-raising flour
1 heaped teaspoon baking powder

pouring cream or crème fraîche, to serve

Preheat the oven to 180°C/350°F/gas mark 4. In a pan, melt the butter, sugar and marmalade for the base, then pour the mixture into the prepared tin. Arrange the orange slices in the tin, overlapping them to cover the whole of the base.

Put all the cake ingredients into the bowl of an electric mixer, sifting in the flour and baking powder last. Turn the speed setting to low, just to incorporate the flour, then increase it to medium and beat the mixture for about 2 minutes, or until fluffy. Spoon the mixture carefully into the tin, making a slight dip in the centre. Place the tin on to a baking tray (to prevent spillage), and bake for 35 minutes. Then cover the top of the cake with a piece of foil to prevent it burning, and bake for a further 25 minutes, or until a skewer inserted into the centre of the cake comes out completely clean.

Leave the cake to cool for about 10 minutes, then slide a knife around the edge, place a plate on the top, turn upside down and release the springs. Serve warm with pouring cream or crème fraîche.

Raspberry Buttercream Cake

This recipe is best served with raspberry iced tea and fresh mint.

Makes **1** cake **GF** Gluten-free **V** Vegan

3 x 22cm baking tins,
greased and floured

For the cake:
225g butter substitute, at
  room temperature
255g evaporated cane
  juice
2 teaspoons vanilla extract
3 cups Gluten-free Flour Mix
  (see below)
4 teaspoons baking powder
6 teaspoons egg replacer,
  whisked with 8 tablespoons
  warm water
240ml soy milk
1 tablespoon white vinegar
125g raspberries, cut into
  quarters

For the buttercream:
225g butter substitute, at
  room temperature
420g organic icing
  sugar
1 teaspoon vanilla extract
2 tablespoons water
  (optional)

Preheat the oven to 180°C/350°F/gas mark 4. Using a hand-held electric whisk, beat the butter substitute, cane juice and vanilla extract at medium speed until combined. Stop and scrape down the sides of the bowl, then turn the mixer to high speed and whip until light and fluffy, about 2 minutes.

Mix the flour and baking powder in a small bowl. In a separate bowl, mix the egg replacer, soy milk and vinegar. Alternate adding the dry and wet ingredients to the mixer bowl, starting and ending with the dry ingredients. After each addition, beat for 10 seconds at low speed, making sure that all the butter substitute is well incorporated. Gently fold the quartered raspberries into the batter, and then pour the batter into the prepared baking tins.

Bake the cake for 22–25 minutes or until a skewer inserted in the centre of the cake comes out clean. Cool the pans on wire racks for 10 minutes, then flip the pans over to release the cakes and cool for another 30 minutes.

Meanwhile, make the buttercream. Using the electric whisk, beat the butter substitute until smooth. Stop and scrape down the sides and bottom of the bowl. Add the icing sugar 140g at a time, mixing on low speed after each addition until well combined. Add the vanilla extract and whip for 1 minute at high speed. If the frosting is too thick to spread, add the water 1 tablespoon at a time. Whip an additional 2 minutes until light and fluffy.

Gluten-free Flour Mix
To make 3 cups, combine 310g white rice flour, 105g potato starch, 40g tapioca starch and 1½ teaspoons xanthan gum, and store in an airtight container in the refrigerator for up to 90 days.

Cranberry Polenta Cake

A delicious gluten-free cake with crunch!

Makes **1** cake   **GF** Gluten-free

20cm loose-bottomed cake tin, greased

125g polenta
250g all-purpose gluten-free flour
1 heaped teaspoon baking powder
150g golden caster sugar
grated zest of 1 orange
150g unsalted butter
1 tablespoon orange juice
1 egg, beaten
1 tablespoon olive oil

For the filling:
250g frozen cranberries
50g demerara sugar
2 teaspoons polenta

cream or crème fraîche, for serving

Preheat the oven to 180°C/350°F/gas mark 4.

Put the polenta, flour, baking powder and caster sugar in a food-processor with the orange zest, and process to combine. Add the butter and process until the mixture resembles fine breadcrumbs. Combine the orange juice, egg and oil and, with the motor running, slowly pour into the processor through the feeder tube.

Once combined, stop the machine and press two thirds of the dough into the prepared tin. Combine all the filling ingredients and pile on to the base, leaving a border of about 1cm around the edge. Crumble over the remaining dough and bake for 45–50 minutes or until golden brown.

Serve warm with cream or crème fraîche.

Lemon, Almond & Pear Cake

This traditional Italian fruit cake is irresistible. Make it in advance and store in a tin for an instant pudding.

Makes **1** cake

20cm springform cake tin,
  lined with baking parchment

250g unsalted butter,
  softened
250g caster sugar
4 large eggs
50g plain flour
250g ground almonds
½ teaspoon almond essence
grated zest and juice of
  2 lemons
4 ripe pears, peeled, halved
  and fanned out
4 tablespoons apricot jam,
  warmed and sieved

Preheat the oven to 180°C/350°F/gas mark 4.

In a bowl cream together the butter and sugar until soft and creamy. Beat in the eggs one at a time adding some flour after each addition. When the eggs and flour have been incorporated fold in the almonds, almond essence, lemon zest and juice.

Spoon the cake mixture into the prepared tin and smooth the surface with the back of a spoon. Top with the fanned out pears. Place in the oven and bake for 1 hour or until a skewer inserted into the centre of the cake comes out clean. If the cake seems to be browning too quickly, cover with a piece of foil.

Glaze with the apricot jam while still warm and allow the cake to cool before removing from the tin.

Cheesecakes

White Christmas Cheesecake

An unctuously creamy white chocolate cheesecake that panders to our aspriations for a white Christmas. This is very much a pudding, and would be delicious served with a little fruit compote, a cranberry one for dramatics.

Makes **1** cake

20cm x 9cm-deep cake tin, with a removable base

For the crust:
50g unsalted butter
150g plain digestive biscuits

For the filling:
4 gelatine leaves
400g crème fraîche
100g white caster sugar
1 teaspoon vanilla extract
75g white chocolate
400g ricotta
white chocolate shavings, to decorate

Gently melt the butter in a small saucepan over a low heat. Place the digestive biscuits inside a plastic bag and crush them to fine crumbs using a rolling pin. Tip them into the saucepan with the melted butter and stir to coat them, and then transfer to the cake tin. Using your fingers or the bottom of a tumbler, press them into the base, making sure you seal the edges, and place in the fridge while you do the next stage.

Place the gelatine in a bowl, cover with cold water and soak for 5 minutes, then drain. Pour 3 tablespoons of boiling water over the soaked gelatine and stir to dissolve. Place the crème fraîche in a small saucepan with the sugar and gently heat, stirring constantly with a wooden spoon until the mixture liquefies and the sugar has dissolved. Give the mixture a quick whisk to get rid of any lumps. It should be warm, roughly the same temperature as the gelatine solution. Stir the gelatine into the crème fraîche mixture, along with the vanilla extract, then transfer to a bowl and leave to cool.

Gently melt the chocolate in a bowl set over a pan with a little simmering water in it. Place the ricotta in the bowl of a food-processor and whizz until smooth; add the melted chocolate and whizz again, then add the cream and sugar mixture and whizz once more. Pour this mixture on top of the cheesecake base. Cover with clingfilm and chill overnight. Decorate with chocolate shavings before serving.

Baked Ricotta Cake

This cake is fantastic because it lasts for 10 days and the flavour gets better as the days go by.

Makes 1 cake

24cm springform tin

400g ricotta
4 eggs, separated
2 tablespoons plain flour
grated zest and juice of
   2 lemons
200g caster sugar
70g butter
12 digestive biscuits, crushed

Preheat the oven to 180°C/350°F/gas mark 4.

Put the ricotta in a bowl and mix in the yolks of the eggs, followed by the flour, lemon zest and juice, and caster sugar. Mix well.

In a separate bowl, whisk the egg whites until stiff peaks form and fold them into the ricotta mixture.

Place a saucepan over a low heat and melt the butter. Once the butter has melted, take the pan off the heat and stir in the crushed biscuits.

Spoon the biscuit mixture into the tin and press it down using the back of the spoon to create a biscuit base.

Pour the lemon ricotta mixture over the biscuit base.

Bake in the oven for 55 minutes.

Once you have poured the cake mixture into the baking tin, cover with fresh blueberries, raspberries or white chocolate drops.

Ricotta & Amaretti Cheesecake

Cheesecake and fruit are great bedfellows. This one, with blackcurrants and raspberries spooned over it, is much lighter than the norm. Contrary to its texture, ricotta has about half the calories of cream cheese.

Makes 1 cake

20cm x 9cm-deep cake
  tin, with a removable base,
  greased

For the pastry:
40g unsalted butter, softened
40g caster sugar
1 large egg yolk
100g plain flour, sifted

For the almond cream:
100g amaretti
40g unsalted butter, diced
1 large egg

For the filling:
3 x 250g tubs of ricotta
225g caster sugar
40g cornflour, sifted
4 medium organic eggs
2 teaspoons vanilla extract
150g fromage frais

250g blackcurrants, removed
  from the vine
200g raspberries

To make the pastry, cream the butter and sugar together in a food-processor until light and fluffy. Beat in the egg yolk, and then add the flour. As soon as the dough begins to form a ball, wrap it in clingfilm and chill for at least 1 hour. You may need to add a couple of drops of water to bring the dough together.

Preheat the oven to 200°C/400°F/gas mark 6. To make the almond cream, place the ameretti in a food processor and reduce to fine crumbs – almost a powder. Add the butter and blend it with the amaretti, then beat in the egg.

On a lightly floured surface, roll out the dough to about 23cm diameter and cut a circle to fit the base of the tin. Press gently into the tin. Spread the almond cream over the pastry and bake for 20 minutes until golden and firm. Remove and allow to cool. Reduce the oven temperature to 190°C/375°F/gas mark 5.

To make the filling, blend the ricotta with 175g sugar and the cornflour in a food-processor for a couple of minutes until very creamy. Now add the eggs, one at a time, the vanilla extract and fromage frais.

Wrap foil around the tin. Pour in the mixture and smooth the surface. Place it in a roasting tray with enough hot but not boiling water to come 2cm up the sides of the tin. Bake for 1½ hours until the centre has set and the top is golden. It may wobble a little if moved from side to side, but should not appear sloppy beneath the surface.

Once cooked, run a knife around the collar, remove it and allow to cool completely. Cover with clingfilm and chill for several hours, or overnight, to allow it to set.

Meanwhile, put the blackcurrants and remaining sugar in a small saucepan and gently heat for a few minutes, stirring occasionally, until the sugar has melted and the currants are almost submerged in juice.

Transfer to a bowl and leave to cool, then stir in the raspberries. You can also prepare the fruit in advance and cover and chill it. Bring back up to room temperature before serving.

Remove the cheesecake from the fridge about 20 minutes before serving with the fruit spooned over.

Triple Chocolate Cheesecake

This is extra delicious served with fresh berries.

Makes **1** cake **V** Vegan

20cm disposable pie dish

For the crust:
10 dairy-free chocolate
   sandwich cookies
½ teaspoon ground coffee
40g tablespoons butter
   substitute, melted

For the filling:
225g tofu cream cheese, at
   room temperature
115g evaporated cane juice
   (or organic whole cane
   sugar if it's not available)
115g tofu sour cream
3 teaspoons egg replacer,
   whisked with 4 tablespoons
   warm water
225g gluten-free chocolate
   chips

For the chocolate glaze:
110g gluten-free chocolate
   chips
2 tablespoons vegan butter
   substitute
1 teaspoon light agave
   nectar
2 tablespoons tofu sour
   cream

Preheat the oven to 180°C/350°F/gas mark 4.

First make the crust. Finely crush the sandwich biscuits in a food-processor for about 1 minute. Pour into a medium bowl and add the ground coffee. Stir in the melted butter substitute. Press the crust into the pie dish.

To make the filling, use a standing mixer to beat the cream cheese until smooth, stopping and scraping down the sides of the bowl as needed. Add the cane juice and soured cream and mix for 1 minute at medium speed. Add the egg replacer and mix for another 30 seconds.

In a microwave-safe bowl, melt the chocolate for 1 minute, stirring after 30 seconds. Remove from the microwave and stir until completely melted. Pour the chocolate into the mixing bowl while the motor is running, then blend on high speed for 1 minute. Pour into the crust. Bake for 25–30 minutes until the filling slightly puffs around the edges and the centre is slightly firm. Cool the pan on a wire rack for 30 minutes. Once cooled, remove the pie plate and place the cheesecake on a serving dish.

Meanwhile, make the glaze. In a microwave-safe bowl, melt the chocolate and butter substitute for about 1 minute. Add the agave nectar and soured cream and stir until combined. Pour over the cooled cheesecake. Refrigerate for at least 4 hours before serving.

Raspberry Ricotta Cake

As lavish as the most extravagant cream cake and worthy of the title 'gateau', this cake is virtually fat-free. It keeps well in the fridge for several days, as the liquid in the ricotta seeps down into the sponge and keeps it moist.

Makes 1 cake

2 x 20cm shallow sandwich or deep cake tins with a removable base, greased

For the ricotta cream:
3 tablespoons seedless raspberry jam
2 x 250g tubs of ricotta, drained of any liquid

For the sponge:
225g hazelnuts, shelled and blanched
4 medium eggs, separated
150g golden caster sugar
1 teaspoon baking powder, sifted

200g raspberries
icing sugar, for dusting

To make the ricotta cream, whizz the jam in a food-processor until smooth, then add the ricotta and whizz again (if you do this by hand, the ricotta will remain grainy). Transfer it to a bowl, cover and chill for several hours, during which time it will firm up a little.

Preheat the oven to 180°C fan/200°C/gas mark 6. Grind the hazelnuts to a powder in a coffee grinder – you will need to this in batches. Whisk the egg whites in a medium bowl until stiff peaks form. In a separate large bowl whisk together the egg yolks and sugar until pale and creamy. Fold the egg whites into the egg and sugar mixture in three goes, then fold in the ground hazelnuts and baking powder. Divide the cake mixture between the two prepared tins, smooth the surface and bake them for 20 minutes until the sponge has begun to shrink from the sides. Run a knife around the edge of the cakes and leave them to cool in the tin.

Remove the collars from the cakes, but you can leave one on the base for ease of serving. Spread half the ricotta cream over this layer to within 2cm of the edge, then sandwich with the other half, gently pressing it down until the cream approaches the edge. Spread the remaining cream on the surface, this time taking it up to the edge, and decorate with the raspberries. Dust them with icing sugar and set aside in a cool place. If keeping the cake longer than a few hours, cover, chill and bring it back up to room temperature for 30–60 minutes before serving.

Vanilla Pumpkin Cheesecake

Garnish this autumnal cheesecake with a ginger biscuit and Coconut Whipped Cream (see opposite).

Makes **1** cake Ⓥ Vegan

dark or silver springform
  cake tin

For the crust:
290g crushed gingersnaps,
  plus 8–10 whole for garnish
35g pecans, chopped
85g butter substitute, melted

**For the vanilla
cheesecake filling:**
675g tofu cream cheese, at
  room temperature
130g evaporated cane juice
  (or organic whole cane
  sugar, if it's not available)
1 teaspoon vanilla extract
4½ teaspoons egg replacer,
  whisked with 6 tablespoons
  warm water

**For the pumpkin
cheesecake filling:**
245g canned pumpkin purée
45g evaporated cane juice
2 teaspoons cinnamon
1 teaspoon pumpkin pie
  spice

Coconut Whipped Cream, for
  garnish (see opposite
  page)

Preheat the oven to 150°C/300°F/gas mark 2 if using a dark springform cake tin, or 160°C/325°F/gas mark 3 if using a silver springform cake tin.

First make the crust. Grind the ginger biscuits in a food-processor until they are finely crushed. Add the pecans and process until just combined. Add the melted butter substitute and mix well. Press firmly on to the bottom and 4cm up the sides of the cake tin.

Next make the vanilla cheesecake filling. Using a stand mixer, blend the cream cheese on medium-high speed until smooth, about 20 seconds. Add the cane juice and mix on medium speed until combined, about 1 minute. Add the vanilla extract and whip for 30 seconds on high speed. Stop and scrape down the sides of the bowl. Add the egg replacer and beat just until blended. Reserve 300ml of the filling in a medium bowl.

To make the pumpkin cheesecake filling, combine all the ingredients. Spoon half of the vanilla cheesecake on to the crust. Top with spoonfuls of pumpkin filling and vanilla filling in repeated layers. Run a knife through the fillings to create a marbled effect. Bake for 45–50 minutes until the centre is almost set. Cheesecake should be custard-like in texture so do not overbake!

Run a small knife between the cheesecake and the tin to loosen the cake, making sure to let it cool before removing from the tin. Refrigerate for at least 4 hours, overnight is best. Garnish each slice with a small dollop of the coconut whipped cream and a ginger biscuit.

Coconut Whipped Cream

Makes 475ml

400ml can coconut milk
35–70g organic powdered
  sugar

Store cans of high-fat coconut milk in the refrigerator at least 8 hour before use. Once chilled, open the cans, making sure not to tilt them over. Remove the lid and scrape the top layer of the coconut fat from the milk layer. Place the coconut fat into a stand mixer. Beat on low speed for 20 seconds. Add the powdered sugar and whip on high for 10 seconds. The mixture should be lumpy. Refrigerate until firm for 1 hour. Whip with a large whisk until the lumps are removed, and serve immediately.

Chocolate
Delights

Chocolate Berry Torte

Makes **1** cake

18–20cm x 6cm-deep cake tin

For the torte:
25g plain flour
5 teaspoons cocoa powder
75g good-quality dark
   chocolate (minimum 60 per
   cent cocoa solids), broken
   into pieces
25g unsalted butter
5 teaspoons double cream
4 egg whites
3 tablespoons caster sugar
3 egg yolks
250g fresh blueberries or
   raspberries
125ml whipping cream, to
   serve

For the icing:
100g good-quality dark
chocolate (minimum 60 per
   cent cocoa solids), broken
   into pieces
50g unsalted butter
3 tablespoons double cream
1 teaspoon icing sugar

whipped cream, to serve

Preheat the oven to 130°C/275°F/gas mark 1. Butter the cake tin and line with greaseproof paper. Sift together the flour and cocoa and set aside.

Melt the chocolate in a heatproof bowl suspended over barely simmering water. Remove from the heat, add the butter and the cream, and stir well until the mixture is quite liquid.

Whisk the egg whites until stiff peaks form, add the sugar and continue to whisk until thick and glossy. Beat together the egg yolks and then gently fold in the flour and cocoa mixture. Add the melted chocolate and mix well. Spoon a few dollops of egg white into the mixture, stir, then gently fold in the remainder of the egg whites.

Gently pour half the mixture into the prepared cake tin, dot half the berries evenly over it, then pour the rest of the mixture on top of the berries.

Bake for 35–50 minutes, until a skewer inserted into the centre of the cake comes out clean. Cool in the tin for 5 minutes then transfer to a wire rack to cool.

To make the icing, melt the chocolate in a heatproof bowl suspended over a saucepan of barely simmering water. Remove from the heat, stir in the butter, cream and icing sugar. Immediately pour over the cake to coat it completely, smoothing the icing using a palette knife. Leave for 1 hour to harden.

Serve with whipped cream and the remaining berries.

Tip: Do not refrigerate this cake once you have iced it as the icing will lose its shine and become dull and lifeless.

Chocolate Mud Cake

This is a very versatile cake, which can be served for dessert or tea. For dessert, serve it barely warm with some tangy crème fraîche and either raspberry purée or a dollop of fresh lemon curd. To serve as a cake, ice with fudge icing and either leave it as is, or drizzle with white chocolate.

Makes **1** cake

24cm loose-bottomed cake tin, buttered and floured

145g unsalted butter
145g plain chocolate (minimum 70 per cent cocoa solids)
145g caster sugar
100ml very hot (but not boiling) water
145g self-raising flour
30g cocoa powder
2 eggs

For the fudge icing:
60g unsalted butter
3 tablespoons milk
200g icing sugar, sifted
30g cocoa powder, sifted

Preheat the oven to 180°C/350°F/gas mark 4. For the cake, place the butter and chocolate in a large bowl. Set over a pan of simmering water and stir well, until melted completely. Remove from the heat and stir in the sugar and hot water.

Sift together the flour and cocoa, then stir into the mixture. Beat in the eggs, one at a time, and mix well. Pour into the prepared tin and level off the top. Bake for 35 minutes, or until a skewer inserted in the middle of the cake comes out clean.

Leave in the tin for 10–15 minutes then transfer to a wire rack to cool before icing. (Or serve warm, as a dessert.) To make the icing, place the butter, milk, sugar and cocoa in a bowl and set over a saucepan of gently simmering water. Stir until the mixture is glossy and smooth.

Remove from the heat and allow the icing to cool completely. Beat well until the cold icing becomes thick, then spread over the cooled cake.

Tip: Chocolate mud cake should only be frozen un-iced.

Chocolate & Brandy Dessert Cake

A crunchy biscuit base and rich chocolatey filling combine to create a deliciously luxurious dessert.

Makes **1** cake **GF** Gluten-free

23cm cake tin, greased and lined with greaseproof paper

75g gluten-free Amaretti biscuits, crushed

400g good-quality dark chocolate (minimum 70 per cent cocoa solids), roughly chopped

4 tablespoons brandy

4 tablespoons liquid glucose

600ml double cream

1 teaspoon cocoa powder

icing sugar and gluten-free Amaretti biscuits, to decorate

Sprinkle the crushed biscuits over the base of the prepared tin. Put the chocolate, brandy and liquid glucose into a bowl and stand over a pan of simmering water. Remove from the heat when the chocolate has melted. Stir well and leave to cool.

Whip the cream lightly and stir into the chocolate mixture. (It is important that the chocolate mixture is not too hot.) Spoon the mixture into the tin, cover and chill for several hours or overnight.

To serve, run a palette knife around the edge of the dessert cake and turn out. Decorate with Amaretti biscuits and icing sugar, and serve.

Chocolate & Ginger Loaf Cake

If you prefer, you could substitute the stem ginger with candied peel or chocolate chips.

Makes **2** 500g cakes

2 x 500g loaf tins, buttered and lined with buttered baking parchment

100g good-quality dark chocolate (72 per cent cocoa solids), chopped
100g plain flour
40g cocoa powder
½ teaspoon baking powder
1 teaspoon bicarbonate of soda
25g ground almonds
pinch of salt
125ml soured cream
75ml sunflower oil
2 large eggs
150g soft light brown sugar
2 nuggets of stem ginger in syrup, finely chopped
50ml boiling water

For the chocolate ganache:
200g good-quality dark chocolate (72 per cent cocoa solids), chopped
75g unsalted butter
2 tablespoons double cream

chopped nuts and stem ginger, to decorate

Preheat the oven to 180°C/350°F/gas mark 4.

Melt the chocolate either in a heatproof bowl set over a pan of barely simmering water or in the microwave on a low setting. Stir until smooth and set aside.

Sift together the flour, cocoa, baking powder, bicarbonate of soda, ground almonds and salt. Mix together the soured cream and sunflower oil. In a bowl of an electric mixer fitted with the whisk attachment, whisk together the eggs and sugar until they are pale and thick and the mixture will leave a ribbon trail when the beater is lifted from the mixture. Stir in the melted chocolate and chopped ginger.

Add the sifted dry ingredients, then the oil and soured cream, and fold into the cake mixture until smooth. Whisk in the boiling water, stir until smooth and divide the mixture between the prepared tins. Bake on the middle shelf of the oven for 35 minutes, or until a (wooden) skewer inserted into the middle of the cakes comes out clean. Cool the cakes in the tins for 10 minutes, then transfer to a wire rack until completely cold.

To make the ganache, melt together the chocolate, butter and double cream either in a heatproof bowl set over a pan of barely simmering water or in a microwave on a low setting. Stir until smooth and combined. Set aside to cool and thicken slightly.

Using a palette knife, spread the ganache over the top of each cake and leave to set before decorating with chopped nuts and stem ginger.

Banana & White Chocolate Cake

White chocolate is one of those things that people either love or loathe, but good-quality chocolate made with real vanilla and cocoa butter will taste very different to the flavour most people are accustomed to.

Makes **1** cake

2 x 18cm cake tins

175g unsalted butter
175g caster sugar
3 large eggs
2 ripe bananas, mashed
250g self-raising flour
½ teaspoon baking powder

For the filling:
2 bananas, sliced
juice of 1 lemon
1 tablespoon rosewater
150ml crème fraîche

For the icing:
200g good-quality white
   chocolate, broken into
   pieces
40g unsalted butter

Preheat the oven to 180°C/350°F/gas mark 4. Brush the baking tins with melted butter and dust with flour. Cream together the butter and sugar, whisk in the eggs and the mashed bananas. Sift the flour and baking powder into the mixture and fold in well.

Divide the batter between the two tins and bake for about 40 minutes. Leave the cakes in the tins for 10 minutes, and then turn out on a wire rack to cool.

To make the filling, toss the sliced bananas in the lemon juice. Mix the rosewater into the crème fraîche and spread this on to one of the cooled cake rounds, top with the sliced bananas and sandwich the two cakes together.

Melt the chocolate and the butter in a heatproof bowl suspended over a saucepan of barely simmering water. Spread the melted chocolate mixture evenly over the top and sides of the cake, starting by pouring it into the centre of the top of the cake and spreading it with a palette knife until it begins to dribble down the sides of the cake.

White Chocolate Goat's Cheese Cheesecake

Use a mild, rindless goat's cheese and vary the fruit according to the season or indeed you taste. Serve with a glass of sparkling wine laced with elderflower cordial.

Makes 1 cake

20cm springform tin

For the cheesecake:
200g chocolate cookies
100g butter
50g demerara sugar
3 free range eggs
200g golden caster sugar
zest and juice of 1 lemon
300g goat's cheese
200g full-fat cream cheese
2 tablespoons cornflour
150g white chocolate, broken
   into pieces

For the raspberry compote:
300g raspberries
100g golden caster sugar
1 teaspoon rosemary leaves
zest and juice of 1 lemon

To make the base for the cheesecake, crush the cookies to the size of breadcrumbs and put in a bowl. Melt the butter and stir into the biscuit crumbs, then add the demerara sugar and mix well. Press the crumb mixture into the tin and allow to cool.

Take a large mixing bowl and whisk together the eggs, sugar, lemon zest and juice, goat's cheese and cream cheese until smooth and lump-free. Add the cornflour and mix well.

Preheat the oven to 150°C/300°F/gas mark 2.

Melt the chocolate carefully in a bain-marie, then slowly pour into the cheese mixture and whisk well. Pour this mixture onto the base and carefully place on a baking tray. Bake in the oven for 1 hour or until golden. The cheesecake should still be slightly soft and have a wobble to the centre when baked. Leaving the cheesecake in the oven too long will cause the cake to crack; overcooking can also cause the filling to go a greeny-grey hue.

Allow the cheesecake to cool thoroughly, then refrigerate in the tin for at least 2 hours.

To make the compote, place the raspberries, sugar, rosemary leaves, lemon zest and juice into a saucepan on a very low heat. cook until soft and deep red in colour. Cool to room temperature.

To serve, remove the cheesecake from the tin and place on a serving plate. Use a hot wet knife to cut perfect and generous wedges, and spoon the compote over the top.

Chocolate, Fig & Almond Cake

This cake is light and moist and the flavour of the chocolate and the almonds together with the texture and taste of the figs combine to make it truly unforgettable.

Makes **1** cake

23cm springform cake tin, greased and lined with baking parchment

150g dried ready-to-eat figs, stalks removed and chopped into very small pieces
3 tablespoons Amaretto
250g unsalted butter
250g caster sugar
75g ground almonds
100g plain flour
4 large eggs
200g good-quality dark chocolate (minimum 60 per cent cocoa solids), chopped
3 heaped tablespoons cocoa powder
100g whole peeled almonds

freshly chopped coconut and whipped cream, to serve

Preheat the oven to 180°C/350°F/gas mark 4.

Place the chopped figs in a small bowl and pour the Amaretto over them. Set aside.

Cream the butter and sugar until light and fluffy. Mix the ground almonds with the flour in a separate bowl. Beat the eggs and add a little at a time to the creamed mixture, beating gently between each addition. (If you are using an electric mixer it should be on its slowest speed.) Then add the almonds and flour a third at a time, continuing to beat gently.

Carefully fold in the chopped chocolate, the figs and Amaretto to the mixture.

Spoon the mixture into the cake tin and smooth over the top using a palette knife. Dust the top evenly with 2 heaped tablespoons of the cocoa. Arrange the whole almonds on top and then bake the cake for 50–60 minutes or until it is firm to the touch and a skewer inserted in the centre comes out clean. Leave to cool and then use a fine sieve to sprinkle the remaining cocoa over the top before serving with some freshly chopped coconut stirred into whipped cream.

Wildy
Decadent

Chocolate Pistachio Orange Cake

Makes **1** cake

For the orange ganache filling:

240ml whipping cream
2 tablespoons golden syrup
1 tablespoon grated orange zest
340g dark chocolate, minimum 50–65 per cent cocoa solids, cut into 5mm pieces
30g unsalted butter, very soft
1 tablespoon orange liqueur
100g candied orange peel cut into 5mm dice

For the orange syrup:

150ml water
70g sugar
2 tablespoons orange liqueur
2 teaspoons vanilla extract

1 batch whipped cream, made with 360ml cream, 2 tablespoons sugar, and 1 teaspoon vanilla extract

1 Pistachio Sponge Cake Layer (page 122)

milk chocolate shavings
candied orange peel
30g blanched pistachios, finely chopped

For the ganache, combine the cream, golden syrup and orange zest in a saucepan and bring to the boil over a low heat, whisking occasionally. Meanwhile place the chocolate in a heatproof bowl. Once the cream mixture boils, pour it through a fine mesh sieve (discard the orange zest) over the chocolate. Wait for 1 minute, then whisk smooth. Cool to room temperature and whisk in the butter, then the liqueur. About 1 hour before you intend to finish the cake, refrigerate the ganache briefly until it reaches spreading consistency.

Meanwhile, for the syrup, stir the water and sugar together in a small saucepan and place over a low heat. Bring to the boil, stirring occasionally. Pour the syrup into a heatproof bowl, cool to room temperature and stir in the liqueur and vanilla.

To assemble the cake, whip the cream by hand or by machine with the sugar and vanilla until it holds a soft peak. Chill in the fridge.

To assemble the cake, use a sharp serrated knife to split the pistachio sponge cake layer horizontally into 2 equal layers. Invert the top of the cake to a cake board or serving plate and use a brush to moisten it with half the syrup. Whisk half the ganache by hand until lightened and spread it on the layer. Scatter the diced candied orange peel over the ganache. Remove the whipped cream from the refrigerator and re-whisk it if necessary. Spread about one third of the cream over the candied peel.

Invert the other layer on to the cream and peel off the paper. Moisten with the remaining syrup. Spread the top and side of the cake with the remaining whipped cream.

Use a palette knife to adhere the chocolate shavings to the side of the cake. Whisk up the remaining ganache and place it in a pastry bag fitted with a 1.25cm star tip (Ateco size 4). Pipe 12 rosettes around the top edge of the cake. Decorate each rosette with a small disc or shred of candied orange peel. Scatter the chopped pistachios all over the top of the cake.

Fudgy Almond Cake with Mint Syrup & Frosting

A great combination of moreish ingredients here – mint, chocolate and honeycomb. Cakes and pastry are notoriously difficult to replicate with gluten-free alternatives but this one is a real winner.

Makes 1 cake GF Gluten-free

24cm x 7cm-deep loose-bottomed cake tin, lined with greaseproof paper

200g unsalted butter
200g gluten-free dark chocolate (minimum 70 per cent cocoa solids), broken into pieces
5 medium eggs, at room temperature, separated
pinch of cream of tartar
240g caster sugar
1 tablespoon vanilla extract
200g ground almonds
50g chickpea (gram) flour

For the syrup:
100g caster sugar
4 tablespoons chopped fresh mint

For the frosting:
500g mascarpone
50g honeycomb, chopped
100g clear honey

Preheat the oven to 180°C/350°F/gas mark 4. Place the butter and chocolate in a heatproof bowl and melt over a pan of simmering water. Once melted, take the pan off the heat but leave the bowl over the pan to keep the mixture warm.

Place the egg whites and cream of tartar in a bowl and whisk until thick and foamy, then add half the sugar, and whisk again until creamy and thick. Add the rest of the sugar and whisk until very stiff, but still a creamy consistency. Stir the egg yolks, vanilla extract, almonds and chickpea flour into the warm chocolate and butter, then straight away add half the meringue, mixing well. Finally, add the rest of the meringue and fold in.

Spoon the mixture into the lined tin and bake for 45–50 minutes, or until well risen and firm. Remove from the oven and cool slightly in the tin; it will collapse a little.

Make several holes over the surface of the cake with a skewer.

Meanwhile, place the sugar, 100ml water and the mint in a small pan and boil until the sugar has dissolved, then strain. Spoon the syrup over the cake and leave to soak in and cool completely. Once the cake has cooled, beat the mascarpone, honeycomb and honey together with a wooden spoon or spatula. Do not whisk or the mascarpone will be too soft and not hold its shape on the cake.

Turn out the cake carefully on to a large, flat plate. As there is no gluten in the cake, it will have quite a soft texture, so be careful. Cover the cake with the honey mascarpone.

Eat straight away or chill for 1 hour. If you want to keep it for the next day, remove from the fridge 1 hour before eating.

Red Berry Pavlova

Snowy white meringue and blood-red strawberries look deliciously dramatic. Within your choice of red fruits, try raspberries, and, if you can get them, some loganberries and wild strawberries.

Makes **1** cake

20cm x 9cm-deep cake tin, with a removable base, lined with baking parchment

For the pavlova:
6 large egg whites, at room temperature
350g caster sugar
1 tablespoon cornflour
1 teaspoon white wine vinegar

For the red berry sauce:
800g red berries, hulled
40g icing sugar
2 tablespoons raspberry eau de vie or kirsch (optional)
squeeze of lemon juice

300ml whipping cream

Preheat the oven to 220°C/425°F/gas mark 7. Cut a circle of baking paper to fit the cake tin.

Whisk the egg whites in a bowl until they rise to a froth. Sprinkle over the caster sugar a few tablespoons at a time, whisking well with each addition. Whisk in the cornflour, then the vinegar. You should have a very stiff, glossy meringue.

Spoon the meringue into the prepared tin and smooth the surface. Place the pavlova on a baking sheet in the oven, reduce the temperature to its very lowest setting and bake for 1½–2 hours keeping an eye on the surface to make sure it doesn't colour. Remove the pavlova and run a knife around the edge of the tin.

Put a third of the berries, the icing sugar, the eau de vie (if using), and the lemon juice in a liquidiser and purée. Pass through a sieve into a bowl, taste and add more sugar or lemon juice as necessary. Halve or quarter any large strawberries and mix the remaining fruit in with the sauce. Remove the collar from the tin and transfer the pavlova to a large serving plate. Whip the cream and spread thickly over the top of the pavlova. Spoon the berries and sauce into the centre with extra around the base if preferred.

Serve straight away.

Mango & Passion Fruit Pavlova

Mango and passion fruit are an excellent combination but it is well worth experimenting with other tropical fruits available in supermarkets.

Makes **1** cake

4 egg whites
pinch of salt
225g caster sugar
1 dessertspoon cornflour
1 teaspoon white wine
  vinegar
250ml double cream
2 passion fruits
3–4 mangoes

Preheat the oven to 120°C/250°F/gas mark ½. Butter a large square of greaseproof paper. Place on a heavy baking tray and dust with a little cornflour.

Place the egg whites and salt in a large bowl. Using an electric whisk beat until they form stiff peaks. Add half the sugar and continue whisking until thick and glossy. This should take 2–3 minutes. Do not be tempted to reduce this time or the finished texture of the pavlova will be spoilt. Add the remaining sugar in a steady stream while continually beating. Whisk in the cornflour and white wine vinegar.

Spoon the meringue mixture on to the baking tray and spread to a rough circle approximately 23cm diameter and 5cm deep. Bake for 1 hour; allow to cool in the oven. Whip the cream to soft peaks. Halve the passion fruit and using a teaspoon scoop out the seeds. Peel the mangoes and cut into long slices. Place the pavlova on a serving dish. Spread the cream over the pavlova. Arrange the mango slices on top and finally spoon over the passion fruit. Chill the pavlova for at least an hour before serving.

Semolina Cake with Honey & Pistachio

Yes, it tastes as good as it looks! Sweet, sticky, and with a little crunch, it is one of the most heavenly cakes you'll ever make.

Makes **1** cake

24cm springform tin, greased

4 large eggs
150g caster sugar
125ml vegetable oil
110g plain flour
110g semolina
1½ teaspoons baking
   powder
pinch of salt
175g pistachios, finely
   ground
1 teaspoon grated lemon
   zest
2 tablespoons pistachios,
   chopped

For the syrup:
300g honey
250ml water
1 tablespoon lemon juice

mascarpone cream, to serve

Preheat the oven to 180°C/350°F/gas mark 4.

Place the eggs and sugar in a large bowl, and beat together with an electric mixer on high speed for about 5 minutes. Reduce the speed and slowly pour in the vegetable oil. Tip in the flour, semolina, baking powder and salt, and mix well until the mixture comes together.

Fold in the ground pistachios and lemon zest. Pour the cake mixture into the prepared tin and bake for 30–35 minutes.

Meanwhile, make the syrup by stirring the honey, water and lemon juice in a saucepan and placing over a high heat. Leave the syrup to boil and reduce by half, which takes about 10 minutes.

Remove the cake from the oven. Use a skewer to poke deep holes in the cake while it is still hot. Drizzle half of the syrup evenly over the top, allowing it to be absorbed, then pour over the remaining syrup. Leave to cool completely, then sprinkle with the chopped pistachios.

Serve with a dollop of mascarpone cream.

Angel Cake

The sweet, vanilla-scented sponge can be made using a decorative kugelhopf tin or a plain ring tin – as long as there's a hole in the centre to allow for quick, even cooking.

Makes **1** cake

1.5 litre kugelhof or ring tin

2 tablespoons vegetable oil
75g plain flour, plus extra for dusting
50g caster sugar
10 tablespoons Splenda granulated sweetener
8 egg whites
1 teaspoon cream of tartar
50g dried skimmed milk powder
1 teaspoon vanilla extract
pulp of 2 passionfruit
a handful of raspberries

For the frosting:
250g mascarpone cheese
300ml double cream
2 tablespoons Limoncello or other citrus liqueur
2 tablespoons lemon juice
1 teaspoon Splenda granulated sweetener

Preheat the oven to 160°C/325°F/gas mark 3.

Brush the tin with the vegetable oil and coat with flour, tapping out the excess. Mix together the caster sugar and sweetener.

Whisk the egg whites in a thoroughly clean bowl until foamy. Add the cream of tartar and whisk again until stiff. Gradually whisk in the caster sugar and sweetener, a spoonful at a time. Stir in the milk powder and vanilla extract. Sift a thin layer of flour over the whisked mixture and fold in using a large metal spoon. Continue to sift and fold in the rest of the flour.

Turn the mixture into the tin and level the surface. Bake for 20–25 minutes until firm to the touch. Loosen the edges of the mould with a knife and invert onto a wire rack. Leave to cool with the tin still in position. (If the cake has risen well above the top of the tin, cut a little off but bear in mind that the cake will shrink back as it cools.) Once cool, transfer to a plate.

To make the frosting, beat the mascarpone in a bowl until softened. Add the cream, liqueur, lemon juice and sweetener and whisk until smooth. Using a palette knife, spread the cream mixture over the cake, swirling it decoratively with the tip of the knife. Scatter the fruits over the top of the cake to finish.

Coconut Macaroon cake

A sponge cake variation on the classic coconut and almond macaroon cookie this cake looks impressive covered with a crunchy topping of desiccated coconut and flaked almonds.

Makes **1** cake

20cm x 5cm-deep cake tin, lined with baking parchment

225g butter
225g caster sugar
4 organic eggs and 1 organic egg yolk
¼ teaspoon pure vanilla extract
225g plain white flour
½ level teaspoon baking powder
25g ground almonds
25g desiccated coconut

For the macaroon topping:
1 organic egg white
10g desiccated coconut
25g ground almonds
75g caster sugar
¼ teaspoon pure vanilla extract
75g flaked almonds

Preheat the oven to 180°C/350°F/gas mark 4.

Cream the butter, add the sugar and beat until light and fluffy. Whisk the eggs and egg yolk and add gradually, beating well between each addition. Add the vanilla extract. Mix the dry ingredients well and stir in gently. Turn into the prepared tin. For the topping, whisk the egg white lightly and fold in the coconut, ground almonds, sugar and vanilla. Spread carefully over the cake mixture in the tin. Sprinkle with flaked almonds and bake in the oven for about 1½ hours or until a skewer inserted in the centre comes out clean.

Cool in the tin, then turn out on to a wire rack.

Tira-Mi-Su Torte

This is one of those rich and glam chocolate creations that will either make a louche tea-time treat or a soignée pud.

Makes 1 torte

20cm x 4cm-deep cake tin, with a removable base

50g self-raising flour
50g light muscovado sugar
50ml groundnut oil
1 medium egg, separated
1 tablespoon espresso, or very strong black coffee, cooled
1 tablespoon full cream milk

For the filling:
300g good-quality dark chocolate, broken into pieces
4 medium organic eggs, separated
30g golden caster sugar
250g mascarpone
2 tablespoons Kahlua or very strong black coffee
edible gold or silver decorations e.g. Smarties, dragées, chocolate stars or leaves

Preheat the oven to 190°C/375°F/gas mark 5 and butter a the cake tin.

Sift the flour and sugar into a medium-sized bowl. Add the oil, egg yolk, espresso and milk, and beat with a wooden spoon until smooth. Whisk the egg white until stiff in another bowl, and fold into the mixture in two goes. Spoon this into the prepared tin, covering the base evenly, and give the tin a couple of sharp taps on the work surface to allow any bubbles to rise. Bake for 12–15 minutes until lightly golden, firm when pressed and shrinking from the sides. Leave to cool.

Place the chocolate in a bowl set over a pan with a little simmering water in it and gently melt. Remove the bowl from the heat and leave the chocolate to cool to room temperature. Whisk the egg whites until stiff in a largish bowl, then whisk the egg yolks and sugar in another bowl until very pale and mousse-like.

Add the mascarpone to the melted chocolate and blend, then fold in the egg yolk mixture, and then the egg whites in two goes. Stir in the Kahlua or coffee. Smooth the chocolate cream over the cake base, cover and chill for several hours or overnight. Decorate with gold or silver decorations, run a knife around the collar of the tin and remove the torte, and serve it in slices.

Panettone

This sweet fruity cake is traditionally eaten in Italy at Christmas time, and is delicious cut into thick slices and served for breakfast with a hot cup of coffee.

Makes **1** panettone

18 cm, deep-sided cake tin, greased with sunflower oil

sunflower oil, for brushing tin
75g raisins
50g candied peel, finely chopped
grated zest of 1 unwaxed lemon
grated zest of 1 orange
125ml milk
10g or 1 level tablespoon active dried yeast
50g caster sugar
450g strong white bread flour, plus extra for dusting
½ teaspoon salt
1 large egg, beaten
1 large egg yolk, beaten
1 tablespoon clear honey
2 teaspoons vanilla extract
75g unsalted butter, softened

For the egg wash:
1 egg yolk
1 tablespoon milk or cream

Tip the raisins into a small bowl, cover with boiling water and set aside for 20 minutes for them to plump up. Drain the raisins and dry on kitchen paper. Mix them with the candied peel and the lemon and orange zest.

Heat the milk until it is warm to the touch and add the dried yeast and 1 teaspoon of the caster sugar. Mix well and leave to one side for 5 minutes to allow the yeast to activate and form a thick foam on top of the milk.

Place 425g of the flour, the remaining caster sugar and the salt into the bowl of an electric mixer fitted with a dough hook. Make a well in the middle of the dry ingredients and add the warm milk and yeast mixture, whole egg and yolk, honey, vanilla extract and softened butter. Mix for about 5 minutes, until the dough is smooth, soft, slightly sticky and elastic. You may need to add a little more flour if the dough is too sticky.

Add the dried fruit and grated zests and mix again until well distributed throughout the dough. Turn the dough out on to a work surface, lightly dusting with flour and knead for 1 minute. Shape the dough into a small ball and place in a large, clean bowl. Cover with clingfilm and leave in a warm, draught-free place for at least a couple of hours, or until doubled in size.

Lightly dust the work surface with a little more flour and lightly knead the dough again for 1 minute. Shape into a ball and place in the prepared tin, smooth side uppermost. Loosely cover with oiled clingfilm and leave for at least 2–4 hours, until the dough is really well risen and has at least doubled in size again. (This will take considerably longer if your kitchen is cool.)

Preheat the oven to 170°C/325°F/gas mark 3. To make the egg wash, beat the egg yolk and milk together and gently brush over the top of the panettone. Using a large sharp knife or scalpel, cut a cross into the top of the loaf and leave it to rise for another 10–15 minutes. Cook the panettone in the bottom third of the oven for about 45 minutes, or until well risen and golden brown. If the top is browning too quickly, turn the oven down slightly for the last 15 minutes of cooking. Leave the panettone to cool in the tin for 5 minutes before turning out on to a wire cooling rack.

To store: Wrapped and placed in an airtight box, it will keep for 1 week.

Darina Allen's Iced Christmas Cake

This makes a moist cake which keeps very well. It can either be made months ahead or, if you are frenetically busy then it will still be delish even if made just a few days before Christmas.

Makes **1** cake

23cm-round or 20cm-square cake tin

110g real glacé cherries, cut in 2 or 4 as desired
50g whole almonds
350g sultanas
350g currants
350g raisins
110g homemade Candied Peel (see opposite)
50g ground almonds
grated zest of 1 organic unwaxed lemon
grated zest of 1 organic unwaxed orange
60ml Irish whiskey
225g butter
225g pale, soft-brown sugar or golden caster sugar
6 organic eggs
1 teaspoon mixed spice
275g flour
1 large or 2 small Bramley seedling apples, grated

Darina Allen's Almond Paste and Cake Icing (page 120)

Line the base and sides of the cake tin with a double thickness of silicone paper. Tie a double layer of brown paper around the outside of the tin, and have another sheet of brown or silicone paper to lay on top of the tin during cooking.

Blanch the almonds in boiling water for 12 minutes, then rub off the skins and chop them finely. Mix the dried fruit, nuts, ground almonds and grated orange and lemon zest. Add about half of the whiskey and leave for 1 hour to macerate.

Preheat the oven to 160°C/325°F/gas mark 3. Cream the butter until very soft. Add the sugar and beat until light and fluffy. Whisk the eggs and add in bit by bit, beating well between each addition so that the mixture doesn't curdle. Mix the mixed spice with the flour and stir gently into the butter mixture. Add the grated cooking apple to the plumped up fruit and stir into the butter mixture gently but thoroughly (don't beat the mixture again or you will toughen the cake).

Put the mixture into the prepared cake tin. Make a slight hollow in the centre, dip your hand in water and pat it over the surface of the cake: this will ensure that the top is smooth when cooked. Now lay a double sheet of brown paper on top of the cake to protect the surface from the direct heat. Bake for 1 hour, then reduce the heat to 150°C/300°F/gas mark 2, and bake for a further 2½ hours, until cooked. Test in the centre with a skewer to see if it is cooked. If so, the skewer should come out clean. Pour the remainder of the whiskey over the cake and leave it to cool in the tin overnight.

Next day, remove the cake from the tin. Do not remove the lining paper but wrap the cake in some extra greaseproof paper and tin foil until required. Store in a cool, dry place; the longer the cake is stored the more mature it will be.

To make the paste and icing, and decorate the cake, see page 120.

Candied Peel

5 organic unwaxed oranges
5 organic unwaxed lemons
5 organic unwaxed grapefruit
1 teaspoon salt
1.3kg sugar

Cut the fruits in half and squeeze out the juice. Reserve the juice for another use, such as homemade lemonade. Put the halves of fruit into a large bowl (not aluminium), add the salt and cover with cold water. Leave to soak for 24 hours.

Next day, discard the soaking water, put the fruit in a saucepan and cover with fresh cold water. Bring to the boil, cover and simmer very gently until the peel is soft, about 3 hours. Remove the fruit and discard the water. Scrape out any remaining flesh and membranes from inside the cut fruit, leaving the white pith and rind intact. Slice the peel into long strips or leave whole if you prefer.

Dissolve the sugar in 700ml of water, bring to the boil, add the peel and simmer gently for about 30–60 minutes, until it looks translucent and the syrup forms a thread when the last drop falls off a metal spoon. Remove the candied peel with a slotted spoon and fill into sterilised glass jars. Pour the syrup over the peel, cover and store in a cold place or in a fridge. It should keep for 6–8 weeks, or longer under refrigeration.

Darina Allen's
Almond Paste & Cake Icing

For the almond paste:
450g golden caster sugar
450g ground almonds
2 small organic eggs
2 tablespoons Irish whiskey
a drop of pure almond extract

For brushing on the cake:
1 organice egg white, lightly
   whisked, or sieved apricot
   jam

For the fondant icing:
1 packet fondant

Sift the caster sugar and mix with the ground almonds. Whisk the eggs, add the whiskey and 1 drop of almond extract, then add to the other ingredients and mix to a stiff paste. Sprinkle the worktop with icing sugar, turn out the almond paste and work lightly until smooth.

Remove the paper from the cake. Put a sheet of greaseproof paper on to the worktop and dust with some icing sugar. Take about half the almond paste and roll it out on the paper: it should be a little less than 1cm thick. Paint the top of the cake with the egg white or apricot jam and put the cake, sticky-side down, on to the almond paste. Give the cake a thump to ensure it sticks and then cut around the edge. If the cake is a little round-shouldered, cut the almond paste a little larger; pull away the extra bits and keep for later to make hearts or holly leaves. Use a palette knife to press the extra almond paste in against the top of the cake and fill any gaps. Then slide a knife underneath the cake or paper and turn the cake the right way up. Peel off the greaseproof paper.

Roll out 2 long strips of the almond paste: trim an edge to the height of the cake with a palette knife. Paint both the cake and the almond paste lightly with egg white or apricot jam. Then press the strip against the sides of the cake: do not overlap or there will be a bulge with the uneven edge upwards. Trim the excess almond paste with a long-bladed knife and keep for decoration. Use a straight-sided water glass to even the edges and smooth the join. Rub the cake well with your hand to ensure a nice flat surface. Leave in a cool, dry place for a few days to allow the almond paste to dry out; otherwise the oil in the almonds will seep through the fondant icing.

To make the fondant icing: Sprinkle a little icing sugar on to the worktop. Roll out the sheet of fondant to a thickness of a scant 5mm. Paint the cake with egg white or apricot jam, then gently lift the sheet of icing and lay it over the top of the cake so it drapes evenly over the sides.

Press out any air bubbles with your hands, then trim the base. Decorate as you wish. Darina uses a little posy of winter leaves and berries, including crab apples, elderberries, rosemary, old man's beard and viburnum. You could also add simple shapes stamped out of the remaining fondant icing – stars, holly leaves, Santas. If you are really creative, the fondant may be coloured using edible food colouring.

Extra Recipes

Maria Elia's Sweet Pastry

Makes 1 x 20cm tart

200g plain flour
70g caster sugar
100g chilled, unsalted butter, diced
2 egg yolks
2–3 tablespoons milk

Mix the flour and sugar together in a food-processor. Add the butter and pulse until incorporated and the mix resembles fine breadcrumbs. With the motor running, add the egg yolks and enough milk to form a soft dough, adding more if necessary. If making by hand, rub the butter into the flour, add the sugar and then bring it together with the egg yolks and milk. Remove the pastry and roll into a ball; wrap in clingfilm and chill in the fridge for 20–30 minutes.

Preheat the oven to 180°C/350°F/gas mark 4. Roll the pastry out between 2 sheets of baking paper (or on a lightly floured surface) until it is large enough to fill the tart case with a slight overhang. Remove the top sheet of the paper and invert the pastry into the tin, paying special attention to the edges. Cut away any overhanging edges, then rest in the fridge or freezer for 15 minutes.

Line the pastry shell with paper, fill with baking beans or rice, place on a baking ray and cook for 10 minutes. Carefully remove the paper and beans and return to the oven for a further 5 minutes or until the base is dry to touch. Leave to cool in the tin.

Sophie Wright's Sweet Pastry

Makes enough for a 22–25cm tart case or 250g of pastry

250g plain flour, sifted, plus extra for dusting
pinch of salt
125g cold butter, cut into pieces
2–3 tablespoons cold water

Mix the flour and salt in a mixing bowl and add the butter pieces. Rub the flour and butter together using the tips of your fingers until it resembles breadcrumbs. Add the water little by little and start to bring the pastry together.

Knead into a ball, cover in clingfilm and put in the fridge for 30 minutes to rest.

Phil Vickery's Gluten-free Flour Mix

Makes 1kg

300g fine polenta or chestnut flour
500g brown rice flour
200g cornflour

Mix all the flours together very thoroughly or put into a food-processor and pulse until mixed. Store in an airtight container.

Extra Recipes

Nick Malgieri's Pistachio Sponge Cake Layer

Makes 1 round layer

23cm round springform tin or
cake tin, greased and lined
with baking parchment

85g blanched unsalted
pistachios
170g sugar, divided
5 medium eggs, at room
temperature, separated
1 teaspoon finely grated
lemon zest
¼ teaspoon finely grated
lemon zest
¼ teaspoon almond extract
pinch of salt
130g plain flour

Set a rack in the centre of the oven and preheat to 180°C/350°F/gas mark 4.

Combine the pistachios and 1 tablespoon of the sugar in the bowl of a food-processor, fitted with the metal blade and pulse repeatedly until the mixture is finely ground. Use a thin palette knife to scrape away any of the mixture caked up in the corner where the bottom meets the side of the bowl. Set aside.

Whisk half the remaining sugar into the egg yolks in the bowl of an electric mixer fitted with the whisk attachment. Whisk the yolk mixture on medium speed until lightened, about 3 minutes. Whisk in the lemon zest and almond extract.

In a clean dry mixer bowl, combine the egg whites and salt. Whisk on medium speed until white and beginning to hold their shape. Increase speed to medium-high and whisk in the remaining sugar 1 tablespoon at a time, continuing to whisk until the egg whites hold a firm peak.

Use a large rubber spatula to fold the yolk mixture into the whisked whites. Then scatter the ground almond mixture over the egg mixture and sift the flour over. Use a large rubber spatula to fold everything together. Work quickly but gently to avoid deflating the batter.

Scrape the batter into the prepared tin and use the spatula to spread it evenly and smooth the top.

Bake the layer until it is risen, golden and firm in the centre, about 30 minutes. Then invert the layer to a rack, leaving the paper on the bottom; place another rack on the layer and invert the whole stack, removing the top rack, so that the layer cools right side up. Cool completely.

To store: Wrap the layer in clingfilm and keep at room temperature until needed, up to 24 hours. Double wrap and freeze for longer storage. Defrost at room temperature for several hours before using.

INDEX

Recipe Acknowledgements

We would like to thank the following authors for kind permission to reproduce their recipes:

Chapter 1: Tarts

p.12 Lemon & Raspberry Tart from *Easy Peasy* by Sophie Wright

p.15 Lemongrass, Ginger & Lime Leaf Chocolate Tart from *The Modern Vegetarian* by Maria Elia

p.16 Treacle Star Tart from *Gorgeous Cakes* by Annie Bell

p.19 Plum, Blueberry & Almond Tart and Plum & Blueberry Jam from *Jams, Jelly & Relish* by Ghillie James

pp.20–1 Toffeed Apple & Pecan Tart and Pâte Sucrée from *100 Great Desserts* by Mandy Wagstaff

p.23 Strawberry Tart from *100 Great Desserts* by Mandy Wagstaff

p.25 Dutch Apple Pie from *Sweet Vegan* by Emily Mainquist

p.26 Crustless Peach & Almond Pie from *Fast & Fresh* by Oded Schwartz and Maddalena Bonino

Chapter 2: Afternoon Tea Cakes

p.30 Madeira Cake from *Forgotten Skills of Cooking* by Darina Allen

pp.32–3 Chequerboard Cake from *Green & Blacks Chocolate Recipes* written and compiled by Caroline Jeremy

p.34 Coffee Cake from *Ballymaloe Cookery Course* by Darina Allen

p.37 Porter Cake from *Ballymaloe Cookery Course* by Darina Allen

p.38 Old-fashioned Victoria Sponge from *Homemade* by Clodagh McKenna

p.41 Citrus Frosted Carrot Cake from *100 Great Desserts* by Mandy Wagstaff

p.42 Seville Orange Marmalade Cake and Seville Whole Orange Marmalade from *Forgotten Skills of Cooking* by Darina Allen

p.45 Frosted Lemon & Lime Drizzle Cake from *Seriously Good! Gluten-free Baking* by Phil Vickery

p.46 Somerset Apple Cake from *On Baking* by Sue Lawrence

pp.48–9 Vanilla & Raspberry Cake from *Seriously Good! Gluten-free Baking* by Phil Vickery

p.50 Roasted Banana Walnut Cake with Maple Icing from *Seriously Good! Gluten-free Baking* by Phil Vickery

p.53 Plum & Almond Butter Cake from *Seriously Good! Gluten-free Baking* by Phil Vickery

p.54 Macadamia, Coconut & Pineapple Cake from *On Baking* by Sue Lawrence

p.57 Cranberry Strussel Cake from *100 Great Desserts* by Mandy Wagstaff

p.58 Cinnamon Spice Plum Cake from *The Modern Vegetarian* by Maria Elia

p.61 Warm Marmalade Upside-down Cake from *Jams, Jelly & Relish* by Ghillie James

p.62 Raspberry Buttercream Cake from *Sweet Vegan* by Emily Mainquist

p.65 Cranberry Polenta Cake from *The Gluten-free Cookbook* edited by Kyle Cathie p.66 Lemon, Almond & Pear Cake from *Easy Italian in Minutes* edited by Kyle Cathie

Chapter 3: Cheesecakes
p.70 White Christmas Cheesecake from *Gorgeous Christmas* by Annie Bell
p.73 Baked Ricotta Cake from *Homemade* by Clodagh McKenna
pp.74–5 Ricotta & Amaretti Cheesecake from *Gorgeous Cakes* by Annie Bell
p.77 Triple Chocolate Cheesecake from *Sweet Vegan* by Emily Mainquist
p.79 Raspberry Ricotta Cake from *Gorgeous Cakes* by Annie Bell
pp.80–1 Vanilla Pumpkin Cheesecake and Coconut Whipped Cream from *Sweet Vegan* by Emily Mainquist

Chapter 4: Chocolate Delights
p.84 Chocolate Berry Torte from *Green & Blacks Chocolate Recipes* written and compiled by Caroline Jeremy
p.87 Chocolate Mud Cake from *On Baking* by Sue Lawrence
p.88 Chocolate & Brandy Dessert Cake from *The Gluten-free Cookbook* edited by Kyle Cathie
p.91 Chocolate & Ginger Loaf Cake from *Gifts from the Kitchen* by Annie Rigg
p.92 Banana & White Chocolate Cake from *Green & Blacks Chocolate Recipes* written and compiled by Caroline Jeremy
p.95 White Chocolate Goat's Cheese Cheesecake from *Adventures With Chocolate* by Paul A. Young
p.96 Chocolate, Fig & Almond Cake from *Green & Blacks Chocolate Recipes* written and compiled by Caroline Jeremy

Chapter 5: Wildly Decadent
p.100 Chocolate Pistachio Orange Cake from *Bake!* by Nick Malgieri
p.102 Fudgy Almond Cake with Mint Syrup & Frosting from *Seriously Good! Gluten-free Cooking* by Phil Vickery
p.105 Red Berry Pavlova from *Gorgeous Cakes* by Annie Bell
p.106 Mango & Passion Fruit Pavlova from *100 Great Desserts* by Mandy Wagstaff
p.109 Semolina Cake with Honey & Pistachio from *Homemade* by Clodagh McKenna
p.110 Angel Cake (© Splenda/McNeil Nutritional Ltd) from *The Sweet Life* by Anthony Worrall Thompson
p.112 Coconut Macaroon Cake from *Ballymaloe Cookery Course* by Darina Allen
p.115 Tira-Mi-Su Torte from *Gorgeous Christmas* by Annie Bell
p.116 Panettone from *Gifts from the Kitchen* by Annie Rigg
pp.118–19 Darina Allen's Iced Christmas Cake and Candied Peel from *Forgotten Skills of Cooking* by Darina Allen
p.120 Darina Allen's Almond Paste & Cake Icing from *Forgotten Skills of Cooking* by Darina Allen
p.122 Nick Malgieri's Pistachio Sponge Cake from *Bake!* by NIck Malgieri

Photography Acknowledgements

We would like to thank the following photographers for kind permission to reproduce their images:

p.2, pp.4–5, p.6, p. 7 William Shaw
p.9 Penny de Los Santos from *Sweet Vegan* by Emily Mainquist

Chapter 1: Tarts
p.13 Kate Whitaker from *Easy Peasy* by Sophie Wright
p.14 Jonathan Gregson from *The Modern Vegetarian* by Maria Elia
p.17 Chris Alack from *Gorgeous Cakes* by Annie Bell
p.18 Laura Hynd from *Jams, Jelly & Relish* by Ghillie James
p.21, p.22 Sara Taylor from *100 Great Desserts* by Mandy Wagstaff
p.24 Penny de Los Santos from **Sweet Vega***n* by Emily Manquist
p.27 William Shaw

Chapter 2: Afternoon Tea Cakes
p.31William Shaw
p.33 Francesca Yorke from *Green & Blacks Chocolate Recipes* written and compiled by Caroline Jeremy
p.35 William Shaw
p.36 Ray Main from *Ballymaloe Cookery Course* by Darina Allen
p.39 Alberto Peroli from *Homemade* by Clodagh McKenna
p.41 Sara Taylor from *100 Great Desserts* by Mandy Wagstaff
p.43 Peter Cassidy from *Forgotten Skills of Cooking* by Darina Allen
p.44 Tara Fisher from *Seriously Good! Gluten-free Baking* by Phil Vickery
p.47 William Shaw
p.49, p.50, p.52 Tara Fisher from *Seriously Good! Gluten-free Baking* by Phil Vickery
p.55 William Shaw
p.56 Sara Taylor from *100 Great Desserts* by Mandy Wagstaff
p.59 Jonathan Gregson from *The Modern Vegetarian* by Maria Elia
p.60 Laura Hynd from *Jams, Jellies & Relish* by Ghillie James
p.63 Penny de Los Santos from *Sweet Vegan* by Emily Mainquist
p.64 Gus Filgate from *The Gluten-free Cookbook* edited by Kyle Cathie
p.67 Gus Filgate from *Easy Italian in Minutes* edited by Kyle Cathie

Chapter 3: Cheesecakes
p.71 Chris Alack from *Gorgeous Christmas* by Annie Bell
p.72 Alberto Peroli from *Homemade* by Clodagh McKenna
p.75 Chris Alack from *Gorgeous Cakes* by Annie Bell
p.76 Penny de Los Santos from *Sweet Vegan* by Emily Mainquist
p.78 Chris Alack from *Gorgeous Cakes* by Annie Bell
p.81 Penny de Los Santos from *Sweet Vegan* by Emily Mainquist

Chapter 4: Chocolate Delights
p.85 Francesca Yorke from *Green & Blacks Chocolate Recipes* written and compiled by
Caroline Jeremy
p.86 William Shaw
p.89 Gus Filgate from *The Gluten-free Cookbook* edited by Kyle Cathie
p.90 Catherine Gratwicke from *Gifts from the Kitchen* by Annie Rigg
p.93 William Shaw
p.94 Anders Schønnemann from *Adventures with Chocolate* by Paul A. Young
p.97 William Shaw

Chapter 5: Wildly Decadent
p.101 Quentin Bacon from *Bake!* by Nick Malgieri
p.103 Steve Lee from *Seriously Good! Gluten-free Cooking* by Phil Vickery
p.104 Chris Alack from *Gorgeous Cakes* by Annie Bell
p.107 Sara Taylor from *100 Great Desserts* by Mandy Wagstaff
p.108 Alberto Peroli from *Homemade* by Clodagh McKenna
p.111 Steve Baxter (© Splenda/McNeil Nutritional Ltd) from *The Sweet Life* by
Anthony Worrall Thompson
p.113 William Shaw
p.114 Chris Alack from *Gorgeous Christmas* by Annie Bell
p.117 Catherine Gratwicke from *Gifts from the Kitchen* by Annie Rigg
p.119 William Shaw